The Economic Theory of Community Forestry

Community forestry is an expanding model of forest management around the world. Over a quarter of forests in developing countries are now owned by or assigned to communities and there is a growing community forestry movement in developed countries such as Canada and the USA. There is, however, no economic theory of community forestry and no systematic treatment of the potential economic advantages of promoting community forestry in developed countries. As a result much of the policy debate over forest management and forest tenure rests on confused and often erroneous views held by policy makers and encouraged by the dominant forestry industry.

The Economic Theory of Community Forestry aims to address this gap and provides the tools for understanding community forestry movement as an alternative form of ownership that can mobilize community resources and encourage innovation. It uses a wide range of economic principles to show how community forestry can be economically superior to conventional forestry, provides examples from Canadian practice, and discusses the regulatory regime that policy makers must put in place to benefit from community forestry.

This book will be of interest to policy makers, activists, community forestry managers and members, foresters and forestry students.

David Robinson teaches resource economics, econometrics and game theory in the School of Northern and Community Studies at Laurentian University in Northern Ontario, Canada.

Routledge Explorations in Environmental Economics
Edited by Nick Hanley
University of Stirling, UK

1. **Greenhouse Economics**
Value and ethics
Clive L. Spash
2. **Oil Wealth and the Fate of Tropical Rainforests**
Sven Wunder
3. **The Economics of Climate Change**
Edited by Anthony D. Owen and Nick Hanley
4. **Alternatives for Environmental Valuation**
Edited by Michael Getzner, Clive L. Spash and Sigrid Stagl
5. **Environmental Sustainability**
A consumption approach
Raghbendra Jha and K.V. Bhanu Murthy
6. **Cost-Effective Control of Urban Smog**
The significance of the Chicago Cap-and-Trade approach
Richard F. Kosobud, Houston H. Stokes, Carol D. Tallarico and Brian L. Scott
7. **Ecological Economics and Industrial Ecology**
Jakub Kronenberg
8. **Environmental Economics, Experimental Methods**
Edited by Todd L. Cherry, Stephan Kroll and Jason F. Shogren
9. **Game Theory and Policy Making in Natural Resources and the Environment**
Edited by Ariel Dinar, José Albiac and Joaquín Sánchez-Soriano
10. **Arctic Oil and Gas** Sustainability at risk?
Edited by Aslaug Mikkelsen and Oluf Langhelle
11. **Agrobiodiversity, Conservation and Economic Development**
Edited by Andreas Kontoleon, Unai Pascual and Melinda Smale
12. **Renewable Energy from Forest Resources in the United States**
Edited by Barry D. Solomon and Valeria A. Luzadis
13. **Modeling Environment-Improving Technological Innovations under Uncertainty**
Alexander A. Golub and Anil Markandya
14. **Economic Analysis of Land Use in Global Climate Change Policy**
Thomas Hertel, Steven Rose and Richard Tol
15. **Waste and Environmental Policy**
Massimiliano Mazzanti and Anna Montini
16. **Avoided Deforestation**
Prospects for mitigating climate change
Edited by Stefanie Engel and Charles Palmer
17. **The Use of Economic Valuation in Environmental Policy**
Phoebe Koundouri

18. **Benefits of Environmental Policy**
    Klaus Dieter John and Dirk T. G. Rübbelke

19. **Biotechnology and Agricultural Development**
    Robert Tripp

20. **Economic Growth and Environmental Regulation**
    Tim Swanson and Tun Lin

21. **Environmental Amenities and Regional Economic Development**
    Todd L. Cherry and Dan Rickman

22. **New Perspectives on Agri-Environmental Policies**
    Stephen J. Goetz and Floor Brouwer

23. **The Cooperation Challenge of Economics and the Protection of Water Supplies**
    A case study of the New York City Watershed Collaboration
    Joan Hoffman

24. **The Taxation of Petroleum and Minerals**
    Principles, problems and practice
    Philip Daniel, Michael Keen and Charles McPherson

25. **Environmental Efficiency, Innovation and Economic Performance**
    Massimiliano Mazzanti and Anna Montini

26. **Participation in Environmental Organizations**
    Benno Torgler, Maria A. Garcia-Valiñas and Alison Macintyre

27. **Valuation of Regulating Services of Ecosystems**
    Pushpam Kumar and Michael D. Wood

28. **Environmental Policies for Air Pollution and Climate Change in New Europe**
    Caterina De Lucia

29. **Optimal Control of Age-Structured Populations in Economy, Demography and the Environment**
    Raouf Boucekkine, Natali Hritonenko and Yuri Yatsenko

30. **Sustainable Energy**
    Edited by Klaus D. John and Dirk T. G. R§bbelke

31. **Preference Data for Environmental Valuation**
    Combining revealed and stated approaches
    Edited by John Whitehead, Tim Haab and Ju-Chin Huang

32. **Ecosystem Services and Global Trade of Natural Resources**
    Ecology, economics and policies
    Edited by Thomas Koellner

33. **Permit Trading in Different Applications**
    Edited by Bernd Hansjúrgens, Ralf Antes and Marianne Strunz

34. **The Role of Science for Conservation**
    Edited by Matthias Wolff and Mark Gardener

35. **The Future of Helium as a Natural Resource**
    Edited by W.J. Nuttall, R. H. Clarke and B.A. Glowacki

36. **The Ethics and Politics of Environmental Cost–Benefit Analysis**
Karine Nyborg

37. **Forests and Development** Local, national and global issues
Philippe Delacote

38. **The Economics of Biodiversity and Ecosystem Services**
Edited by Shunsuke Managi

The Economic Theory of Community Forestry

David Robinson

LONDON AND NEW YORK

First published 2017
by Routledge
2 Park Square, Milton Park, Abingdon, Oxon, OX14 4RN

and by Routledge
711 Third Avenue, New York, NY 10017

First issued in paperback 2018

Routledge is an imprint of the Taylor & Francis Group, an informa business

© 2017 David Robinson

The right of David Robinson to be identified as author of this work has been asserted by him in accordance with sections 77 and 78 of the Copyright, Designs and Patents Act 1988.

All rights reserved. No part of this book may be reprinted or reproduced or utilised in any form or by any electronic, mechanical, or other means, now known or hereafter invented, including photocopying and recording, or in any information storage or retrieval system, without permission in writing from the publishers.

Trademark notice: Product or co=ay be trademarks or registered trademarks, and are used only for identification and explanation without intent to infringe.

British Library Cataloguing in Publication Data
A catalogue record for this book is available from the British Library

Library of Congress Cataloging in Publication Data
Names: Robinson, David, 1947 February 22- author.
Title: The economic theory of community forestry / David Robinson.
Description: Abingdon, Oxon ; New York, NY : Routledge, [2016] | Includes bibliographical references and index.
Identifiers: LCCN 2016006779 | ISBN 9781138100725 (hardback) | ISBN 9781315657516 (ebook)
Subjects: LCSH: Community forestry–Economic aspects. | Forests and forestry–Economic aspects. | Forestry and community–Economic aspects.
Classification: LCC SD393 .R63 2016 | DDC 333.75–dc23
LC record available at https://lccn.loc.gov/2016006779

ISBN 13: 978-1-138-59933-8 (pbk)
ISBN 13: 978-1-138-10072-5 (hbk)

Typeset in Palladio
This book has been prepared from camera-ready copy provided by the author.

Contents

List of Figures	ix
List of Tables	xi
Foreword	xiii
The Plan of the Book	xvii

I	**OVERVIEW**	1
1	What is Community Forestry?	3
2	Traditional Territories, Industrial Forestry, and the Community Forest	13
3	Tenure, Property Rights, and Community Rights	23

II	**ECONOMICS**	39
4	Forests and Joint Production	41
5	Human Capital and Social Capital	55
6	The Efficiency of Community Forestry	67
7	Externalities and Community Forestry	81
8	Public Goods and Public Forests	91

viii   *Contents*

III   COMMUNITY — 101

9   Transaction Cost Theory and Community Forestry — 103

10   The Creative Potential of Community Forestry — 117

11   Coops, Worker-Managed Firms and Community Forests — 133

12   Community Forestry and the Professional Forester — 141

13   Conclusions and Policy Advice — 151

Appendices — 159

A   A Brief Introduction to Traditional Forestry Economics — 161

B   Time and Natural Resource Decisions — 179

C   Definitions — 185

Bibliography — 189

Index — 203

List of Figures

1   Community forestry and related fields   xviii
2   How the chapters are related   xix
3   The economics section   xxi
4   The community section   xxii

2.1   The imaginary uninhabited forest   13
2.2   The inhabited forest with community territories   14
2.3   The inhabited forest as part of a nation state   15
2.4   State timber leases unrelated to traditional uses   17
2.5   Redrawing the map around communities   18

3.1   The political economy of a two-product forest   26

4.1   Joint products   41
4.2   Forests as a system of joint products   43
4.3   Value-added counted in six stages of production   45

5.1   A simple material culture   57
5.2   A modern capitalist culture   59

6.1   Portrait of Vilfredo Pareto (1848–1923)   68

8.1   Public and private goods   91
8.2   Public spectacles are public goods   92
8.3   Bill's indiviudal demand for streetlamps   95
8.4   Sue's individual demands for streetlamps   96

x *Figures*

8.5 Summing the individual demand curves   97

9.1 Transaction costs may exceed the value of a transaction   104
9.2 Hypothetical management units and transactions   107
9.3 Transaction costs decline with vertical integration   107
9.4 Transactions costs with mergers   108

10.1 A network graph   117
10.2 A multi-product, multi-interest forest   119
10.3 A hierarchical network   121
10.4 A simple lattice   122
10.5 A small world graph and a random graph   123
10.6 Sample history of job creation   126
10.7 Time steps to find all innovations   127
10.8 Comparing losses   129

12.1 Supply and demand for foresters   143

A.1 Marginal and total product curves for a timber stand   164
A.2 Maximum mean annual increment   167
A.3 Maximizing net revenue   168

B.1 Discounted value of $100   179
B.2 Continuous and discrete discounting   182

List of Tables

2.1 Forest ownership   14
2.2 Arguments for community forestry   19

3.1 Inefficiencies in private forest tenures   28
3.2 Ten possible reasons why tenure reform is not needed   36

4.1 Selected ecosystem services   48
4.2 Valuing unpriced services   51
4.3 Market and non-market values   52

10.1 Joint distribution of jobs and string lengths   124

12.1 Aspects of the practice of forestry   144

13.1 Six features of the ideal community forestry tenure   155

A.1 Content of an introductory course in forestry economics   163
A.2 Some determinants of the value of a tree   165

Foreword

This is a book about a field that doesn't exist. It was started to solve a problem that does exist – that the rapidly developing community forestry movement had no answer to questions like "Could community forestry ever be as efficient as conventional industrial forestry?"

That there was a gap in economic theory became clear in the face of a disastrous decline in forest production in the early part of the 21st century; mills were shutting down and forest communities were losing jobs and people. Many activists were arguing for increased community control. They met resistance from forestry companies, ministry officials, and sometimes local politicians.

Opponents of local control often made economic arguments that had no empirical support. In effect, their arguments amounted to "We have always done things this way and we know best. Forestry markets are good because markets in general are good". To an economist, the arguments against local control appeared to be at best ill-founded and, at worst, self-serving. It seemed a good time to look carefully at the economic potential of community forestry.

Dipping into the forestry literature showed that researchers had long been suggesting that community forestry should be given a chance.[1] The UN and an array of non-governmental agencies were actively promoting community forestry.[2] Many countries, including Indonesia, India, the Philippines, Mexico, Brazil, and Nepal had extensive community forestry programmes. In the economics literature there was research suggesting decentralization is likely be more efficient than centralized management, but there were no articles in

xiv *Foreword*

the literature investigating whether community control could be as efficient or economically superior to the dominant industrial model.[3]

It might be that the answer seemed obvious: how could anyone argue that a move from professional management by large companies to local management by amateurs could do anything but introduce massive inefficiencies? Although local control of the forest might result in slightly more sensitive ecological management, and might resolve some minor local conflicts with tourism or access to hunting and fishing, surely small-scale community enterprises would result in higher costs and fewer jobs?

This study is focussed on community forestry for developed countries and for boreal regions. While an estimated 300 million[4] people worldwide living close to tropical forests depend on tree or forest products for daily subsistence (Pimentel et al., 1997), two-fifths of forest exports come from just two 'developed' countries, Canada and the United States. Forests and forest communities in these countries, like others in the developed North, differ greatly from those in the tropical developing countries.[5] The forest residents are wealthy by world standards and have experience with a variety of stable and fairly efficient democratic institutions. Markets are efficient, productivity is generally high, and property rights are well defined. As Mallik and Rahman (1994) explain, community forests in developed countries are usually large, capital intensive and market oriented. Community forestry in this context obviously differs from what has emerged in the developing regions.

There is a distinct lack of economic analysis for the northern nations. Community Forestry in the developed north will involve new contractual arrangements, new interpretations of individual and collective rights with respect to local forests, new marketing arrangements, new specialized education for management, new opportunities for foresters, and expansion of silvicultural techniques to adapt them to multi-product, new intensive local forestry techniques, new innovation in labour markets, new techniques for collaboration, new training in democratic planning, and new applications of economic theory for the evolving institutions. A better understanding of the relevant economic theory, which this book tries to provide, can help support emerging community forest organizations and can help to frame the legislation to support them.

Organizations calling for governments to increase communities' role in forest management

- Center for International Forestry Research (CIFOR)
- Convention on Biological Diversity (CBD Secretariat)
- Food and Agriculture Organization of the United Nations (FAO)
- Global Environment Facility (GEF Secretariat)
- International Tropical Timber Organization (ITTO)
- International Union for Conservation of Nature (IUCN)
- International Union of Forest Research Organizations (IUFRO)
- United Nations Convention to Combat Desertification (UNCCD Secretariat)
- United Nations Development Programme (UNDP)
- United Nations Environment Programme (UNEP)
- United Nations Forum on Forests (UNFF Secretariat)
- United Nations Framework Convention on Climate Change (UNFCCC Secretariat)
- World Agroforestry Centre (ICRAF)
- World Bank

Notes

[1]"Policy inquiries repeatedly find that forest-dependent communities ought to have a stronger role in determining their relations with the surrounding forests". (Duinker et al., 1994)

[2]In British Columbia, for example, local control was endorsed in the 1945 and 1956 Sloan Commissions on the forest resources (Harshaw, 2000).

[3]"Transfers in forest tenure to families and communities through the process of devolution have been accompanied by a growing predominance of forest production and processing by communities and smallholders in the forest products and service industries (Molnar et al., 2011). This has been the case in Bolivia, China, Guatemala, Honduras, India and Mexico (Macqueen and Team, 2010) and Peru, Ecuador, Burkina Faso, Gambia, and Papua New Guinea (Donovan et al., 2006)". (Vega and Keenan (2014))

[4]According to the International Union for Conservation of Nature, a total of 1.6 billion people depend on forests for their livelihoods. About 1.4 billion of these live in the developing world, and 1 billion live in extreme poverty.

[5]For tropical regions,"The community forestry development models require a local adaptation to a set of practices, customs, and rules that are not only alien and difficult to comprehend and absorb, but they also conflict to an important degree with local moral-economic principles". Jong et al. (2010)

The Plan of the Book

The Economics of Community Forestry is about forest production and community production. It draws on a wide range of subfields in economics, including network theory, the theory of the worker-managed firm, models of joint production, analysis of economies of scope and scale, human capital theory, and theories of economic development. The resulting combination is itself a new sub-field  of economics containing the tools needed to promote an efficient, fair and resilient forestry sector. This book attempts to pull together the main elements of that largely unexplored field.

Simply adding the word "community" to forestry complicates things enormously, as many professional foresters have discovered. Forestry Economics is a well developed field with a long tradition and sophisticated mathematical models. There are excellent textbooks available and courses are offered in most or all Forestry Schools. The Economics of Community Forestry is much broader, however. As a result much of the material in the core economics sections of this book does not appear in typical forestry economics courses.

The economics of community forestry employs tools already incorporated in forestry economics, such as optimal rotation theory, cost-benefit analysis, environmental economics and rent theory. It also requires specific tools from distributional theory, economic development, human capital theory, information economics, public goods theory, the theory of externalities, principle agent theory and the theory of social capital. Figure 1 illustrates some of the subfields in economics that contribute techniques to the economics of community forestry.

The economics of community forestry is not simply a subfield of forestry economics. It is perhaps more accurate to think of forestry economics as a subfield of community forestry.

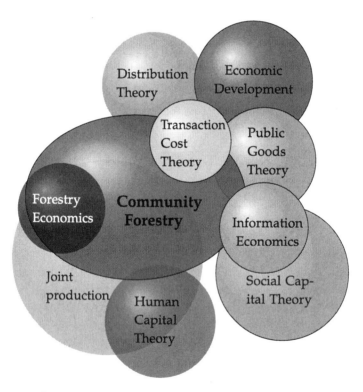

Figure 1: Community forestry and related fields

0.1 A Map of Topics

Figure 2 is a map of the major topics. The chapters naturally fall into three large blocks. The first block includes interrelated chapters on history, tenure and a discussion of the nature of community forestry.

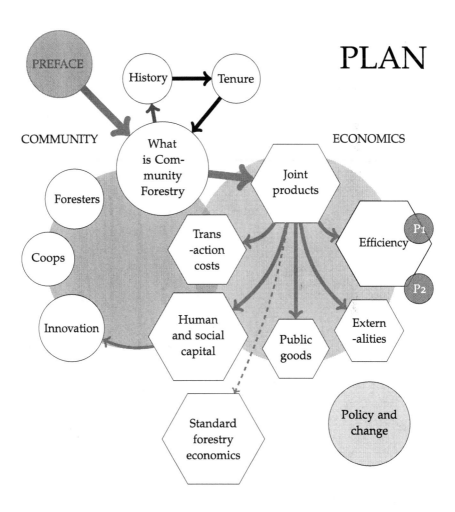

Figure 2: How the chapters are related

xx *The Plan of the Book*

The second block is the core of this book. It contains a series of chapters, each dealing with a core economic concept as it applies to community forestry. The third block deals more directly with the community part of community forestry. The book can be read in almost any order. Figure 2 also suggests some of the more obvious sequences, as well as some of the most important links between chapters.

0.2 History and Definitions

The first chapter in the introductory section defines community forestry and identifies the pure model of community forestry that the book deals with. It provides background, establishing basic concepts linking community and economic theory. A chapter on history and territory explains that community forestry is not really new. A chapter on tenure and the problem associated with tenure provides the institutional context. Tenure is an allocation of property rights, and any allocation of property rights is highly political. A move to community forestry is essentially a type of land reform. Since the forests are publicly owned, however, the reform is a matter of decentralizing government rather than expropriating property.

0.3 Theory

The 'theory' chapters are designed to give forestry decision-makers and activists the economic language they need to hold their own in policy discussions. Chapters are written to be accessible to non-economists, but they should also be useful for many economists and economics students because they apply standard theory to an unfamiliar problem. Some equations are included, as much to help non-economists understand the weird ways of economists as to convince economists that the arguments are tightly connected to standard economic theory. Chapters are intended to be self-contained and can be read in any order. Many include illustrative diagrams.

The chapters in this block may be useful for professional foresters

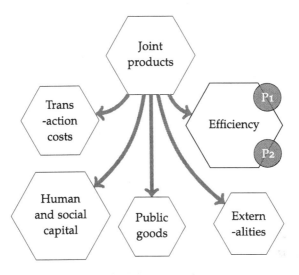

Figure 3: The economics section

in particular, since they present the economic theory that justifies many of the claims and objectives of the proponents of community forestry. Experts around the world suggest that professional foresters are encountering community forestry more and more, and that the concerns of the community forestry movement are increasingly central to the profession.

Chapter 4 on joint products (two or more outputs generated simultaneously, by a single manufacturing process using common inputs) is the gateway to the economics section. The concept of joint products provides the opportunity to examine forest communities as part of the forest ecosystem. This system-level view reveals why community forestry provides improved incentives for forest management. A simple two-output model shows why the interests of a community forest organization would be better aligned with the interests of the public than are the interests of a conventional profit-maximizing forest company operating under the current tenure system. The concept of value-added is introduced. Since many products of the forest are not sold in the market there is a section on valuing non-marketed

xxii The Plan of the Book

goods and a discussion of environmental services.

The concept of capital is a basic tool of economic analysis. In Chapter 5 a section on the varieties of capital provides a brief critical introduction to the theory of capital for anyone who wants to understand how community forestry differs from conventional industrial forestry. Sections on human and social capital provide the strongest link between community and the economics of the book. Both are byproducts of forestry and goals for communities.

Efficiency is a central concept in economics. A chapter on efficiency should either come before all the others as preparatory material or at the very end as reference material. It ended up in the middle of the book because it presents two general propositions that in a real sense lie behind many of the the arguments in the rest of the book.

Chapters 7 and 8 introduce externalities and public goods, two key ideas in economics that are especially relevant for community forestry.

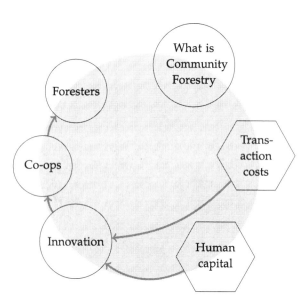

Figure 4: The community section

0.4 The Community in Community Forestry

Community forestry is more than a transfer of ownership to local communities: it involves, and even demands, a very different form of social organization. Chapter 9 on transaction cost theory provides the necessary concepts.

Chapter 10 on the innovation potential of community forestry applies network theory to see how a change from corporate forestry would affect employment and community well-being. Corporate forestry is modelled as a hierarchical network and community forestry quite naturally fits the description of a small world network. Chapter 11 explores self-management as an approach. Chapter 12 is of primary interest for professional foresters. It tries to answer the question "What would happen to the forestry profession with a major expansion of community forestry?"

Appendix A presents core results from Forestry Economics. It is written primarily for non-foresters. It is presented as an appendix because it is relatively technical and because the material is covered in much greater detail in standard works. The appendix may serve as a useful review for some professional foresters

Part I

OVERVIEW

1
What is Community Forestry?

> "The case for real local control in forest policy, particularly for those at the short end of labour-shedding 'efficiencies' and monopoly control, has always been strong".
> Lawson, Levy, and Sandberg, 2001

Any forestry scheme in which the local community plays a significant role[1] in forest management can be – and probably has been – called community forestry. The communities involved range from urban neighbourhoods in developed countries to Brazilian indigenous peoples.
Institutional forms that are called community forestry range from committee-run neighbourhood parks through multi-level consultative processes to outright community ownership.[2] The local communities may be defined as 'stakeholders' or rights owners. Not surprisingly, the academic literature provides many definitions of community forestry.[3]

Rather than deal with the economics of everything that can be called community forestry, the book explores a special, pure model. For us,

> Community forestry is a decentralized and democratic form of public ownership of forests. In this stylized pure type, a resident community effectively owns the local forest, it depends on the forest for a significant fraction of its living, it makes all the important decisions about forest resources, and it captures all the benefits from forest use.

4   *What is Community Forestry?*

This definition is more limited than some in the literature and less restrictive than others. The definition is much much more restrictive than, for example, the definition Glasmeier and Farrigan (2005) derive from a 'metastudy of the concept': "At its essence, community forestry involves some form of participation and self-awareness on the part of stakeholders and is geared toward sustainable outcomes with at least some additional benefits gained by the local population".

Community forestry was initially defined, by FAO, as "any situation which intimately involves local people in a forestry activity. It embraces a spectrum of situations ranging from woodlots in areas which are short of wood and other forest products for local needs, through the growing of trees at the farm level to provide cash crops and the processing of forest products at the household, artisan or small industry level to generate income, to the activities of forest dwelling communities"

FAO, 1978.

Crucially, the definition used in this book is less restrictive than some because it does not prescribe any goal or purpose for community forestry.[4] As McDermott and Schreckenberg (2009) observe, "Scholars and proponents may layer on additional features that they take to be necessary qualifications for community forestry, such as commitments to equitable participation, environmental improvement or social wellbeing". Pagdee, Kim, and Daugherty (2006), for example, claim that, "Theoretically speaking, the definition of CFM's success should integrate out-comes of ecological sustainability, social equity, and economic efficiency in which objectives for long-term use of the resources are well defined so that expectations of users and the society at large remain consistent".[5]

The version of community forestry that we explore in this book is centred on effective local ownership, which implies both control and capturing benefits, and on democratic forms. The economic potential for community forestry stems from these structural features and not from intentions.

Decentralized control and democratic decision-making drive the results in this book. Decentralization allows management that takes account of local features – the fine details of soils, climate topography and of the local workforce. In principle a decentralized management supports diversification and a sensitive response to local needs and opportunities. Decentralization also may encourage innovation, as Chapter 10 demonstrates.

Democratic decision-making has at least three important economic consequences. The first is that it naturally takes into account the needs and desires of the people involved. Second, democratic decision-making is likely to use the knowledge and skills of the community more effectively that any form of top-down management. Finally, democratic decision-making is likely to develop individual talents and community capacity.

1.1 The Community Forestry Solution

The emphasis on a resident community makes this a "place-based" approach to governance. Harrington, Curtis, and Black (2008) and others (e.g., Duane (1977)) argue for an alternative approach to natural resource management based on interests. Ostrom et al. (1999) and others argue that because resource management problems appear at multiple levels, a multi-level governance system is needed, including interests and capacities situated outside of the local communities. Mill operators similarly argue they should be represented in decision-making. The arguments are valid, especially with transboundary resources like water, migratory species like fish, or industries that

6 *What is Community Forestry?*

pollute. The argument is much less compelling in the case of remote forest-based communities. Spillover effects are more clearly limited and more likely to be internalized by resident forestry communities. Multiple use tends to be largely by local populations. Furthermore local communities have a continuing interest: they can be expected to outlast most corporations, politicians and environmental organizations.

In any case, the question is not whether non-local interests should be heard. For community forestry, the question is at what level should the primary rights be vested and who should make the final decisions after proper consultation. This book explores the economic implications of vesting the rights at the level of the local community. The community does not have to be a cohesive 'organic whole' with well-developed decision-making capacity before we undertake this analysis.[6] On the contrary, it is more likely that vesting rights at the local level will create or increase community cohesion and capacity.

1.2 Boundaries

The concept of community is more than a little tricky when linked to the word 'forest'.[7] The reason is that the expression 'community forest' implies much more than simply an abstract association of people. The expression 'community forest' signals the right of a specific group of people to make decisions about, and to appropriate the returns from, a specific forest. It is about power and income, two very contentious matters.[8]

Defining the community for community forestry means making three boundaries explicit. The jurisdictional boundary defines the powers that the community can exercise, the spatial boundary defines a territory, and the social boundary defines membership. These are all political questions.

1.2.1 Jurisdiction

The ultimate owners of most of the world's forests are nation states, so community forestry can only work where the state devolves its interest to a local community. In many cases – for example in most of Canada's huge boreal forest – people living in forested regions, deriving a significant fraction of their collective income from harvesting or managing the local forest, and sharing many interests, pursuits and occupations, currently have no legal right to make decisions about the forests they depend on. They also have no right to any residual income from forest production. Those rights are held by provincial or national governments and they are delegated to forest companies. Where there are populations of aboriginal descent those communitiees may have achieved or may be struggling to achieve some control of forests they inhabit. Their demands are supported by now widely recognized notions of aboriginal rights.

Since formal control of production and the right to allocate any surplus are the primary features of ownership (Hansmann, 1988), community forestry is an alternative form of public ownership.[9] Seeing community forestry as a form of public ownership suggests that perhaps all members of the local community should be shareholders and/or equal voting members, creating something like a cooperative or a municipal corporation. This raises a variety of issues. The most important may be whether a collective governance can be economically efficient.

Often local institutions are not equipped to deal with conflicting claims on the resource from disparate user communities and external stakeholders. They may not be equipped to handle or manage a forest (Bradshaw, 2003). Lack of capacity may lead to economic inefficiency and is likely to result in control being captured by minority interests. Devolution should therefore be accompanied by a determined and intelligent strategy for local capacity building at the community level.[10]

Setting these issues aside for now, there is an important point that follows directly from the definition of community forestry used

8 *What is Community Forestry?*

here. As a first approximation, the interests of the community are likely to be close to the interests of the general public, as represented in theory by senior government. A community dependent on the local forest would therefore voluntarily operate roughly the way that the larger community would desire. The principal agent problem is minimized by devolution. Both regulation and oversight are cheaper when the incentives of the agent are reasonably well aligned with those of the principal. Community forestry thus has the potential both to represent the public interest in a locally sensitive manner and to resolve some of the conflicts inherent in the joint product-high externality nature of forestry. In doing so it takes on some of the roles of higher level government. This provides a basic theoretical argument for local control of forests.[11]

1.2.2 *Spatial Boundaries*

A negotiation-based approach to settling spatial boundaries is suggested briefly in Chapter 2. The process is likely to be complicated because it will need to take into account geographical and environmental features, economic interests and traditional territorial claims. The resulting boundaries are likely to be disputed under community forestry, as they are disputed in any regime.

1.2.3 *Membership*

It seems likely that permanent residency will be the primary basis of community membership in most cases. For aboriginal communities, tribal membership may prevail. Cottagers clearly have a property interest that sometimes conflicts with the economic interests of permanent residents. Hunters, fishers, campers, hikers and canoeists have legitimate interests as well. Chapter 9 on transaction costs suggests that rights can be distributed in many ways and still yield efficient outcomes if rights are clearly defined and protected and the cost of negotiating with rights-holders is low. Assigning rights to local residents is likely to be the clearest and simplest arrangement and therefore likely to minimize transaction costs.

Community forestry as a growing phenomenon *Community Forestry as a Growing Phenomenon* 9

There are other issues, including: what happens when the labour force is reduced or when people join or leave the community; should children be members or be allowed to become members; what rights employees resident elsewhere have; whether additional shares can be bought; what is the community objective function; how should decision-making be arranged; will such an arrangement encourage innovation; can the arrangement achieve efficiency; and how should the entity relate to harvesters and mill workers. All of these issues would reward detailed analysis, and several have been dealt with, to some extent at least, in literature on firm ownership, cooperatives, and worker-managed firms.[12]

1.3 Community Forestry as a Growing Phenomenon

Community forestry as an institutional form is expanding around the world. It has been developing most rapidly where there are indigenous forest populations but it is also expanding in some developed countries.[13] In Quebec, Ontario and New Bruisesswick public policy actively supports the creation of community forests. Duinker et al. (1994), writing of Canada more than 20 years ago, observed that that, "The apparent growing interest in community forests ... has opened an exciting and challenging frontier for forest interests. We are convinced that Canada's future will be characterized by increases in people's demands for community forests, and by more experiments and trials to test a variety of manifestations of the concept".

In developing countries, community forestry is mainly linked to meeting basic needs. In the US it is primarily about democratic participation in discussions about the use and management of the forest resource (Glasmeier and Farrigan, 2005). The driving forces are environmental organizations and in some cases anti-poverty programmes. Community forestry in the US has had the committed financial support of philanthropic organizations like the Ford Foundation "interested in promoting grassroots-based efforts to develop integrated solutions to environmental and social problems" (Moote and Becker, 2004). According to Charnley and Poe (2007), "there has been resistance to, and lack of political support for, giving communities tenure rights to public forests on the part of government and environmental groups. Constraints include Aboriginal constitutional issues, legal barriers, fear that community control will cause forest degradation, and concern that community management will favour local over national interests in public lands".

Two distinct processes are expanding the domain of community forestry in Canada. One is the increase in land under First Nations management. The second is increasing provincial government support for community forestry in British Columbia. There are now 125 community forests across Canada. In Australia, community forestry is a new concept and literature on the topic is limited (Charnley and Poe, 2007).

Community forestry is said to have, in general, three benefits: it is equitable, supports diversified economic development, and is thought to be good for the environment. There is evidence for all of these propositions (Bray et al., 2003; Schusser, 2012).[14] Community forestry is rarely presented as a serious economic challenge to large-scale industrial forestry. Economic theory suggests, however, that community forestry can be economically superior to industrial forestry and can deliver benefits that industrial forestry cannot.

Notes

[1]"The definitions of community forestry are as numerous and varied as the communities trying to implement them". Gunter and Ambus (2004)

[2]"A community forest can be described as any forestry operation managed by a local government, community group, First Nation or community-held corporation for the benefit of the entire community". British Columbia Community Forest Association

[3]Community forestry as a policy issue arises out of the forestry profession's efforts to set up a new partnership with local people and to respond to the subsistence needs of growing rural populations. (FAO 1978).

[4]Baker and Kusel (2003) identified community forestry's objective as being "to conserve or restore forest ecosystems while improving the well-being of communities that depend on them".

[5]For a discussion of definitions that supports this approach here, see Rath (2010).

[6] 'More often than not, community represents heterogeneous values, beliefs, norms and interests signifying difference, contestation and conflict across space and time. (Harvey (1996), cited in Harrington, Curtis, and Black (2008)).

[7]**Community:** a social group of any size whose members reside in a specific locality, share government, and often have a common cultural and historical heritage. OED

[8]"Community is what people who care about each other and the place they live create as they interact on a daily basis". (Flint, Luloff, and Finley (2008))

[9]A firm's "owners," as the term is conventionally used and as it will be used here, are those persons who share two formal rights: the right to control the firm and the right to appropriate the firm's residual earnings. (Hansmann (1988))

[10]"Is it right and necessary for communities to 'go it alone'? Can governments provide support by, for example, aiding with capacity-building in those cases where such capacity appears limited?" (Bradshaw (2003))

[11]"It can certainly be hoped and often expected that many resource-dependent communities, were they to gain management authority for local resources, would be credible in the exercise of their new powers, given their attachment to place and their desire to persevere in that place". (Bradshaw (2003))

[12]See, for example, Miyazaki and Neary (1983) for a suggestive example.

[13]In 2005 Glasmeier and Farrigan (2005) analyzed 250 cases covering more than 60 countries: "The contribution from the United States was the greatest (18%) followed by developing countries where community forestry has been formally engrained and where it is the most extensive (e.g. Nepal 11%; India 11%; the Philippines 5%)". In BC there are 57 organizations representing nearly 90 communities. 51 have negotiated long-term Community Forest Agreements.

[14]"Community forestry holds promise as a viable approach to forest conservation and community development" Charnley and Poe (2007)

2

Traditional Territories, Industrial Forestry, and the Community Forest

> "The history of humans, is a story of forests and their use. Trees have provided the principal fuel and building material of human societies since prehistoric times."
> FAO's 2012 report on the State of the World's Forests

The FAO State of the Forest Report for 2001 opened by noting two seemingly opposite trends in the forest sector: localization and globalization. Many countries were decentralizing the responsibility for forest planning and management while facing the impacts of expanding global trade and globalization. Community forestry is a version of decentralization in which power over the forest and returns from the forest are devolved to democratic local forest communities. The community remains and the global markets remain, but direct control by the national state is reduced. It represents a reversion to an earlier norm of local control.

Figure 2.1: The imaginary uninhabited forest

The return to local control is combined with more formally specified democratic norms, and it occurs in the context of global markets

	Public	Private
Centralized	~60%	0%
Decentralized	~20%	18%

Source: Grebner et al (2013) p79

Table 2.1: Forest ownership

and culture. Community forestry is at once a relatively new idea and a modern version of the traditional relationship between people and their forests. To provide some context for the discussions in the rest of the book, this chapter presents a brief history of forest governance and an argument for the reinstatement of community forestry given that history.

2.1   The Forest: An Ecosystem with People

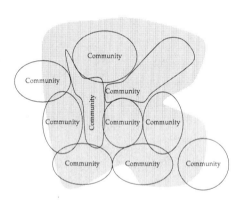

Figure 2.2: The inhabited forest with community territories

The forest ecosystem is an ecosystem with people. A forest without people (Figure 2.1) is an abstraction at best and is a misrepresentation of the ecology of most of the world's forests. For most of the time that people have lived with, in, and near forests they have depended on the forest for sustenance, but they have also made decisions about managing the forest around them. Figure 2.2, illustrating an inhabited forest, is a much better conceptual map for thinking about forests and forestry.

Figure 2.2 illustrates what might be thought of loosely as the political geography of 'traditional forestry'. The forest is partitioned into territories used by and in certain senses controlled by and owned by a resident population. Community territories were probably flexible and determined though interaction with neighbouring communities. Though many communities had established family or clan rights, control was largely exerted by the community rather than through private ownership. In modern terms, the forest was usually common property, used according to sets of rules that had evolved locally and which generally, but not always, achieved reasonable efficiency, sustainability, and security for the community. Elinor Ostrom and her colleagues have documented some of the ways that local communities have successfully regulated forests and other resources (Ostrom et al., 1999).

In general forest peoples relied on very specific local knowledge to provide foods and other goods that were produced and transformed using traditional techniques. Populations were regulated by the carrying capacity of the forest itself. Some forest territories supported hunter-gatherer societies, some communities progressively cleared their territories, and some evolved into larger territorial systems that supported towns and even cities.

Between the diverse traditional forms of forest tenure and modern community forestry lies a period of in-

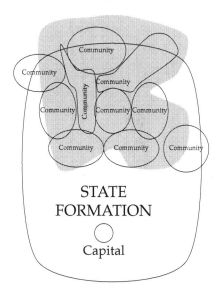

Figure 2.3: The inhabited forest as part of a nation state

creasingly centralized control by nation states. The development of the modern state brought varied traditional cultures and communities under overarching legal and property systems. The established arrangements of the inhabitants were often ignored and went unrecognized. Communal territories often became state property.

According to Whiteman, Wickramasinghe, and Piña (2015), the proportion of forest owned by the state has fallen slightly from 85% in 1990 to 82% in 2010, and privately owned forests have increased in importance from 14% to 18% of the total forest area over the same period. Some of the public forests are protected areas, some support local populations, some are subject to intense predation and overuse, others are given over to the commercial production of timber and pulp. In principle, all of these forests are managed for the public good. Precisely how these public assets should be managed is an important question.

Having extended control over forest regions, states often went on to allocate harvest rights over nominally state properties without consulting local populations. In many colonies local administrations supported themselves with resource fees, or the sale of property belonging to the state, and drew boundaries for logging rights arbitrarily (Figure 2.4).

The result was to create an industrial form of forest tenure that had little or no relationship to traditional communities and that extracted wealth on behalf of metropolitan owners. In North America, for example, immigrant workers created new logging towns tied to world trade networks in the territories of hunter-gather societies. In India local capitalists often destroyed forests that had supported local communities for centuries. Local institutions withered or were simply replaced by central control.

2.2 Forest Regimes Today

In democratic states a curious dual structure of power has emerged. Typically small and remote forest communities are weakly represented in state governments. Traditional and aboriginal communities

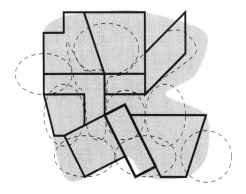

Figure 2.4: State timber leases unrelated to traditional uses

may not be represented at all. Democratic institutions for managing forests, if they exist, are typically highly attenuated.[1]

Forests, on the other hand, are generally allocated and regulated by a ministry of the state government. Local employees of timber companies are directed by local managers but have little or no say in the management of forests. Companies deal with the ministry directly and the ministry reports to a minister who might or might not be part of a democratically elected government. Effective power lies in the combination of ministry and company interests. The result can be rapid deforestation, as in Indonesia, according to the World Resources Institute (WRI),[2] Deforestation is a consequence of state control of the forests. According to the WRI: "Deforestation in Indonesia is largely the result of a corrupt political and economic system that regarded natural resources, especially forests, as a source of revenue to be exploited for political ends and personal gain."

Guiang et al. (2001) claim that the dismal performance of the state in forest governance was one of the factors leading to the emergence of community forestry or community-based forest management in the Philippines. Both indigenous peoples[3] and migrants had been "the subject of government neglect and gross injustice for a long time either through inequitable resource allocation, or outright displacement by favoured logging or mining concessionaires."

Company ownership might be local, especially early in the process, but companies often merged and increasing ownership is global. India's Aditya Birla Group, for example, has two mills in New Brunswick and one in Ontario, Canada. Nippon Paper Industries and the Marubeni Corporation of Japan own a pulp mill in Alberta. Mercern owns pulp mills in Germany and British Columbia. Canfor Pulp Limited Partnership, the largest North American – and third largest global – producer of pulp and the leading producer of Kraft Paper, has operations in Canada, and the eastern USA, with sales offices across Europe and Asia.

Many countries are now decentralizing the responsibility for forest planning and management even as they face expanding global trade and globalization. Community forestry is a version of decentralization in which power over the forest and returns from the forest are assigned to democratic communities. It represents a reversion to an earlier norm of local control combined with more formally specified democratic norms in the context of global markets and culture.

2.3 Implications for Community Forestry

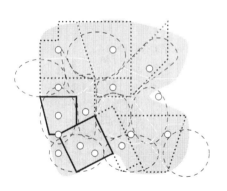

Figure 2.5: Redrawing the map around communities

Decentralization and community forestry would require redrawing the tenure maps, taking into account both traditional territorial boundaries where they are still relevant, watersheds and natural boundaries, and the natural economic zones of the current communities. Figure 2.5 illustrates a situation in which forest jurisdiction has been reassigned to resident communities.

Table 2.2: Arguments for community forestry

1. performance of the state in forest governance has been dismal;
2. forest resource allocation appeared to favour more the rich than forest-dependent communities;
3. forest-dependent communities have a larger stake in sustainable forest management as their survival is dependent on this resource base;
4. local communities have better knowledge and understanding of the terrain, the resources, their constraints and opportunities;
5. many forest-user groups have developed knowledge systems and institutions that allow them to regulate local forest use;
6. when decisions, programmes and projects are done by those who should know them best (the people themselves), responsiveness, effectiveness and efficiency optimally obtained;
7. forest protection and sustainable use are more effectively achieved when local communities plan and implement these themselves;
8. local communities are in a better position to respond to such emergencies as fire outbreaks, encroachment, or timber poaching;
9. both indigenous peoples and migrants have been the subject of government neglect and gross injustice for a long time either through inequitable resource allocation, or outright displacement by favoured logging or mining concessionaires;
10. community forestry is viewed as a concrete effort to realize the national ideals of democracy and social justice.

Source: Guiang, Borlagdan, and Pulhin (2001)

The resulting territories are unlikely to correspond closely to traditional territories of course. Territories have always been somewhat flexible and often contested. Even today overlapping claims are not uncommon, at least in Canada. In many countries a significant fraction of the indigenous populations have moved to new communities based on modern resource extraction. Immigration has added non-indigenous population, and these people have often been resident for generations. There will be no allocation that satisfies every legitimate claim.

A democratic response to the conflicting claims suggests that new boundaries should be established by the people with current and historic claims. Senior governments can support the science needed to make good decisions and can mediate, but ultimately communities are best placed to decide based on local knowledge, traditional knowledge and science.

Some elementary principles are likely to apply. Territories should probably be large enough to support existing forest-dependent communities. Some communities are less dependent on forest resources and will need less territory. Modern transportation systems have replaced traditional routes and the boundaries of new jurisdictions should probably be influenced much more by the technologies in use than by historic modes.

Whatever rules emerge, the process is likely to be time-consuming. The process of negotiating boundaries will strengthen community identities and help to develop their capacity for self-governance.

2.4 The Re-emergence of Community Forestry

Local control of ecosystems is the historic norm. Local control of land is the the norm in modern agriculture. In forestry, local control has not been the norm in the age of the nation state. It is now, however, expanding around the world.

Community forestry has been developing most rapidly where there are indigenous forest populations. Guiang, Borlagdan, and Pulhin (2001) have examined the reasons leading the government

The Re-emergence of Community Forestry **21**

of the Philippines to support community forestry. Many of their observations also apply in the developed world.Their review of the literature on the Philippines produced the list in Table 2.2

Community forestry is also expanding in some developed countries. Duinker et al. (1994), writing of Canada more than 20 years ago, observed that that "The apparent growing interest in community forests ... has opened an exciting and challenging frontier for forest interests. We are convinced that Canada's future will be characterized by increases in people's demands for community forests, and by more experiments and trials to test a variety of manifestations of the concept." More recently, and taking a more global perspective, Charnley and Poe (2007), among others, have argued that "community forestry holds promise as a viable approach to forest conservation and community development."

An extensive body of work by Ostrom and others demonstrates that communities have successfully managed resources in the past and continue to do so in many places. Castén (2005) suggests that management by the adjoining communities may in fact be the most cost-efficient way of managing a forest.

Notes

[1]Community organizations have had to negotiate a range of institutional and regulatory constraints that make their activities and operations unnecessarily difficult and unsustainable. (Dressler, McDermott, and Schusser, n.d.)

[2]"Indonesia is in transition from being a forest-rich country to a forest-poor country, following the path of the Philippines and Thailand." World Resources Institute (WRI)

[3]Indigenous communities, peoples and nations are those which, having a historical continuity with pre-invasion and pre-colonial societies that developed on their territories, consider themselves distinct from other sectors of the societies now prevailing on those territories, or parts of them. From the UN Study on the Problem of Discrimination against Indigenous Populations. (Cobo, 1982)

3
Tenure, Property Rights, and Community Rights

Ownership is a social relationship: society accepts and usually helps enforce a specific set of rights, called property rights, for the owner. The 'economics of community forestry' is about the economic possibilities when a resident community effectively owns the local forest. This chapter is about what it means for a community to effectively own a forest.

Ownership is a bundle of rights that can be enforced. The rights may include

1. the right to use the property
2. the right to make decisions about the property
3. the right to appropriate any income from or products of the property
4. the right to exclude others from the property
5. the right to transfer the property

When these rights have been defined for a particular segment of the world – a piece of land, a building, an idea or even a financial derivative, and when the defined rights are given to or taken by a person, group or corporate body, that segment of the world is a property.

24 *Tenure, Property Rights, and Community Rights*

Possessing property, and possessing the associated rights cannot be separated.The specific rights can be separated or limited, however. Owners may rent their property, giving up the right to use it and make certain decisions about how it will be used. They may not be allowed to use urban properties for farming chickens. Electric power companies may have the right to cross, park on, or even modify private property to maintain transmission lines. Owners may be able build on a piece of land but may not be allowed to change the water flow, fill wetlands or grow marijuana. Property taxes and stumpage fees may take some of the income. Hunters or hikers may have a right to cross private property using traditional trails. Leaseholders may have all the rights of a property owner except the right to sell.

> **Tenure:** The conditions under which land or buildings are held or occupied. From Old French tenir 'to hold', from Latin tenere.

Tenure is a broad term used to refer to control of land, forests or other resources: resource tenure shapes the organization of production, the distribution of benefits, and the pattern of economic and social development (Ostrom, 2005). Not surprisingly, the way forest resources have been made available to timber enterprises has always been at the centre of the debate on forest policy (Zhang and Pearse, 1997). Tenure has both economic and stewardship implications. Without secure rights, forest users have few incentives – and often lack legal status – to invest in managing and protecting their forest resources. While secure property rights cannot ensure sustained protection and investments in an asset, the absence of clearly defined rights can open the way to over-exploitation and underinvestment.

Forest tenure usually includes the right to cut a specific amount of timber in a specified area during a given period, often with additional restrictions designed to protect environmental resources, and with replanting requirements. Conditions of tenure may include a requirement that plans be presented, that mills be operated, roads maintained, and access for other users be provided. There may be conditions under which the tenure reverts to the state. Tenure may or may not be transferrable.

The dominant tenure system in much of the developed world is rooted in a particular historical context. Governments that found themselves owning large areas of forest often adopted a policy of allocating forest rights to harvesters in exchange for government revenue. In the settler states of the 'New World', forests were uninhabited from the Crown's point of view. Uninhabited really meant there were no important political actors. Indigenous populations were generally discounted or ignored. Only the timber values and the crown revenue mattered. As Stephen Harvey (1996) observed, the interests of the Crown and the timber companies were well aligned. Both wanted to maximize revenue from the timber harvest. In many, even most, cases Crown and company were not even clearly separated.

3.1 Regulatory Problems

As Luckert (2009) puts it "Market/Private interests do not always coincide with public interests." Governments have developed a complex system of regulations to reduce infringements on the public interest by forest tenure-holders. The regulatory structure itself introduces new inefficiencies. Some of these are listed in the box on page 28.

Figure 3.1 illustrates some of the difficulties that arise when forest rights are assigned to private interests. The figure describes the trade-off between just two goods. All the feasible combinations of recreation and timber that can be produced by a local forest are shown as a shaded area. Any point in the shaded area is possible, so the region is called the "feasible set".

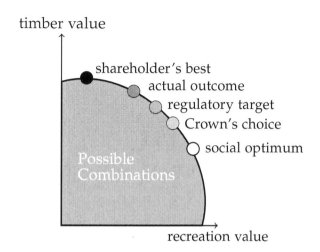

Figure 3.1: The political economy of a two-product forest

Not all the combinations are equally attractive. If a community were producing inside the feasible set it would always be possible to increase the output of timber or recreational services or both. The efficient combinations of timber and recreation that can be produced are shown as the dark curved line (known as a "production possibility frontier" or PPF).

From the points of view of a shareholder in a company holding a timber lease, value is increasing in the vertical direction. The shareholder is only interested in timber harvest. The shareholder gets no benefit from recreational services provided by the the forest. The shareholder would expect the company manager to choose the mix of products labelled "shareholder's best".

For society as a whole in this story, timber and recreational services are both valuable. The Crown might prefer to shift production to the point labelled 'Crown's choice', near the social optimum. The Crown's choice is often influenced by consultations with 'stakeholders', and the most easily identified stakeholder with the largest financial interest in the choice is likely to be the firm already holding tenure rights. It is also influenced by its own regulatory personnel, who typically have worked closely with tenure holders for many years and who often move between public service and industry. When members of a regulatory agency created to act in the public interest become so attached to the commercial or political concerns of special interest groups that effectively act on behalf of the regulated we have what George Stigler (1971) called *regulatory capture*.[1] The theory of regulatory capture has been since been extended (Laffont and Tirole, 1991) and has become an essential tool for understanding issues like tenure reform.

When regulators have been 'captured', the targets set by the Crown may diverge from the social optimum. The targets that can be achieved by the resulting regulations, the 'regulatory target' in Figure 3.1, may then fall short of the government's goals.

Regulation imposes 'compliance costs' on firms. The firm would, of course resist even a limited impact on its profits. In practice a company will often stop short of what regulations call for, although may argue that it has in fact complied. Shading compliance in this way is to be expected because there is often a great deal of money at stake.

Regulation also requires monitoring and enforcement expenditures by government. Enforcement is costly and government enforcement might be weak. Rigorous enforcement might incur high legal costs.

In general, if the public wants a small deviation from profit-making behaviour, the cost of regulation is small, but large adjustments can be very costly. Although in Figure 3.1 the result is nowhere near the social optimum or even the Crown's original target, even weak regulations weakly enforced provide an increase in the desired recreation services.

Figure 3.1 illustrates economic positions that could be political targets and/or compromises. They share an economic feature: they are all efficient, all 'on the production possibility frontier'. The negotiations involved in reaching an allocation do not guarantee that efficiency will actually be achieved, however.

Table 3.1: Inefficiencies induced by the need to regulate private forest tenures

1. Reduces profitability, flexibility, and is costly to administer.
2. Creates a situation in which agents are economically disconnected from the consequences of at least some of their actions (the externality problem). Decisions made by an agent with partial rights are unlikely to be economically efficient.
3. Projects that generate a net benefit for society may not be undertaken because the net benefit for the rights holder is insufficient.
4. Partial rights systems impose regulatory and transactions costs.
5. As the number of claims on the forest increases, the problem becomes more complex and, in fact, less amenable to market solutions through privatization.
6. The Sustained Yield framework focusses entirely on timber production.
7. Non-timber resources are treated as harvesting constraints, rather than joint products to be optimized.
8. The Allowable Cut Effect (the increase in today's average annual allowable cut attributable to expected future increases in yields) provides an incentive to plant faster growing trees on land subject to an Average Allowable Cut to benefit from the immediate increase in the ACE that results.
9. Zhang and Pearse (1997) report, similarly that the form of tenure influences the reforestation rate, with more secure and comprehensive tenure being associated with more complete reforestation. The general principle is the assignment of rights and the associated harvest constraint may shape tomorrow's forest.
10. Changing the sustainability targets for wildlife requires changing regulations for wood harvest because the licensee does not have economic incentives for performance with respect to wildlife.
11. The effort to stabilize the harvest of a single class of forest product may gradually destabilize the ecological system. Holling (1973) and Holling (1986)
12. A "use it or lose it" provision may force production when market conditions would suggest stopping production. This is particularly so for economically marginal forests.
13. Appurtenancy requirements, where they exist, require a licensee to construct, modify or maintain a timber processing facility. Forestry firms are thus forced to become vertically integrated.

The list of problems here draws heavily on a presentation by forestry analyst, Luckert (2009), at the 2009 Conference of the Ontario Professional Foresters Association.

3.2   Three Challenges for a Forest Tenure System

Assigning tenure rights solves or partially solves a number of problems. It provides security for producers, giving them confidence that they can earn a return on their investments. It reduces the transaction costs involved in managing the forests, as outlined in Chapter 9. It gives the tenure-holder an incentive to maximize the value of their forest rights, which in principle could maximize the value of the forest to society.

There are three major problems in assigning tenure that have not been solved in the existing system, however. These are the joint-production problem, the discounting problem and the community development problem.

3.2.1   Joint Production

The joint production problem is the most fundamental of the three. Wood is easily the most important revenue generator in a forest economy, but the forest also supplies a range of other products and services, such as water storage and filtration, carbon sequestration services, canoe routes, owl habitat. Economists speak of joint production in cases like this. Baumgärtner, Faber, and Schiller (2006) argue that "joint production" of this sort is the structural cause behind modern-day environmental problems. Harvesters and mill owners do not earn revenue for the services of the forests in cleaning water or sequestering carbon, and as a result they will take these products into consideration only out of goodwill or because of regulation. The main argument for privatizing forests, in fact, is that a private owner with the right to exploit every aspect of the forest might take all of the values into account.

Joint production is discussed in more detail in Chapter 4, where a case is made that community forestry would avoid many of the problems that arise with private tenure.

30 *Tenure, Property Rights, and Community Rights*

3.2.2 *Discounting*

The discounting problem arises because the future intrudes into almost every forest management decision. The forest is a capital system; its value is derived from the expected value of the flow of services far into the future. Appendices A and B lay out the way the value calculations and discounting are usually presented in forestry economics. The important point, however, is that estimates of economic value are filtered through the rights of the different players. If tenure-holders discount the future services of the forest excessively, they are likely to under-invest in the future of the forest and to over-exploit the standing resource.

Unfortunately it is almost impossible to make the case that international corporations discount at the optimal rate for the general public, or that corporate shareholders have the same time preferences as local residents. The discount rates used by firms are effectively determined by capital markets and commercial interest rates.

Many economists are convinced that the rate at which people discount their future health, the children's well-being and the health of the forests should either be aligned with the market rates or will naturally come to be aligned with market rates. In that case discounting exponentially at the market rate makes sense. Others argue that there are reasons, moral, empirical and logical, not to discount at market rates and not to employ constant discount rates. See Price (2011) for a discussion of variable-rate discounting in the context of the forest planning. The argument for community forestry in this case is that resident communities are likely to discount differently than non-resident firms and shareholders do.

It is important to understand that the rate of return on financial capital does represent a genuine opportunity cost that should be considered in making decisions. When, for example, we ask if we should cut a tree today or let it grow for another year, we need to balance the growth and other benefits of postponing the harvest against the income we could generate if we sell the tree and invest the money. Unfortunately the real market return is not a well-defined concept. The market offers different rates to borrowers and lenders, to large and small borrowers, to governments and the poor. Financial institutions can collapse before paying out on long-term deposits and short-term rates of return vary. Inflation rates are uncertain, so any fixed rate is also uncertain in real terms. The logic of using the market rate is clear, but which rate to use is not.

3.2.3 Development

The third major issue in the design of a tenure system has to do with developing human and community capacity. Responsibility is fundamental to the development of human capacity. Other things being equal, a tenure system that involves more people in decision-making is a better system. Involving people is costly, however. It requires taking time, sharing information, and developing expertise and decision-making skills.

For a forestry company there may be advantages to public participation, but in most cases, public participation is a cost. Modern management is designed to economize on intelligence and attention precisely because they are among the most valuable and costly resources a company can have. For the community these costs are both investment in correct decisions and investments in human development, similar to educational expenditures. Chapter 5 examines how community forestry contributes to the production of human and social capital.

3.3 The Community Forestry Solution

A direct approach to the problem of ensuring decisions are consistent with the public interest might be to hand control of the forest over to the local community. This is the community forest approach. It solves the three challenges described in Section 3.2 by creating an appropriate decision-making body.

32 *Tenure, Property Rights, and Community Rights*

3.3.1 *Joint Production with Community Forestry*

Community forest tenure can and should give the community forest organization control of an extended set of the potential joint products. This is likely to be politically acceptable because both democratization and decentralization have positive values in the political culture. The community then has an incentive to use those rights efficiently and the general interests of a resident community will generally align roughly with the public interests. Providing that they can also achieve efficient outcomes, community forestry would therefore serve the public interest better than either forests run by the companies or forests managed by the Minister of Natural Resources.

Luckert (2009) has questioned whether the interests of communities are sufficiently aligned with those of the general public for community forestry to result in good management decisions. It is a question difficult to answer without a clear model of what is meant by interests and how they relate to decisions. We argue that the answer is obvious once the interests and production possibilities are modelled as in Section 3.1.

3.3.2 *A Tilt Toward Conservation*

There is a simple structural reason why communities are likely to come close to what the wider public wants. It seems likely, for example, that conservationist sentiments are as common in forest communities as in the general populations. With industrial tenures these sentiments act on the firm from outside through moral pressure and regulation. In a democratic community organization these sentiments work from inside the decision-making councils. The democratic nature of a community forest tends to align the interests of the organization with goals of the larger community. The principle applies as well for other decisions.

Unlike a regulatory solution, a community-based solution represents an internal equilibrium, with some members wanting to, for example, increase production and other wanting reductions. The resulting choice will tend to be stable. In a regulatory solution the firm wants more production and the regulators are supposed to resist that pressure. The regulators, however are not easily observed and not directly accountable to the public. Their interests tend to become aligned with those of the regulated firm (Stigler, 1971; Laffont and Tirole, 1991). The "regulatory target" of Section 3.1 is not stable. Regulatory regimes have a tendency to drift toward the solutions preferred by the most influential players.

The conflict between the public, with its concern for conservation, and the firms that act on the natural world can be reduced with community forestry. That is one reason why conservation organizations tend to support community forestry initiatives around the world.

3.3.3 Discounting Differently

Residents who are likely to have children in the community, who have established homes, and who have developed friendships and community-specific social capital are likely to care about the long-term condition of the forest they depend on. Community forest organizations are therefore likely to behave as though they were discounting the future differently from the way firms would.

There is a struggle, both in the theoretical literature and in society at large, over how heavily future benefits should be discounted. Community forestry does not solve the problem. It shifts the political balance in decision-making for one relatively small segment of the economy. Forestry, however is an enterprise in which the social discount rate affects almost every decision. With community forestry discounting becomes a matter for community decision and community choice.

3.4 Human Development

Certainly community decision-making will involve costs and conflict. It will be necessary to invest time and money in providing information, recording decisions, and facilitating public meetings. Two considerations are relevant. First, community decision-making

34 *Tenure, Property Rights, and Community Rights*

and participation will make new resources available for forest management – time and intelligence that is not available in the current system or that is used in oppositional ways. These resources are not costless in the broadest sense, but society is likely to be better off if they are directed toward solving communal problems.

Second, and this is extremely important, energy and time spent managing communal forests will *produce* social capital: it is not simply a cost. The management of community forests will develop more people with management skills and knowledge that can be used to promote the community. Community forestry itself is a form of joint production, with social capital the invisible and potentially undervalued second product.

Fundamentally it is people who produce wealth. The most important investment a government can make is in people. This view is understood when we talk about the public education system. Universities increasingly see co-op programmes that give students practical experience as an effective way to create capacity. Traditional apprenticeships relied on on-the-job training. Management recruiters look for students with experience in the non-profit sector and in promoting community projects. Community forests would create valuable management capacity, which would increase wealth-creation capacity.

A concern for human development provides an answer to another question raised by Luckert (1999). Why bother maintaining forestry communities that developed to serve an industrial mode that no longer needs them? After all, a sentimental concern for a dying way of life may be a poor guide to forest policy. The answer is not that the communities in some sense deserve special exemption from the forces of the market. The argument rests on the value of these communities to the rest of society. These communities can be a place where human talents are developed, although the existing tenure system is a barrier.

3.5 Conclusion

Ideally the choice of a tenure regime should take into account all costs and benefits, monetary and otherwise, to the communities, the forest companies and to society at large under the alternative regimes. Unfortunately the data is not available.[2] There is far too little historical data on alternative tenure systems to make a data-based choice.

Furthermore, valid experiments are not possible: is it likely that any experiment would have demonstrated that the prototype for the Blackberry could challenge Bell's established telephone system? Policy makers would have had to compare an imagined regime – a hypothetical world – with the world they knew.

It is possible to use economic theory to test a number of hypotheses about the current tenure system, however. Consider the ten propositions listed in Table 3.2. If these hypotheses are accepted based on available evidence, there would be no reason to consider community forestry. On the other hand, if the hypotheses lack support, there would be no reason to resist community forestry.

There is no evidence to support **Hypothesis 4** that industrial forestry expands value-added production. In Ontario, for example, industrial tenure holders are known to resist allocating unused wood supply to new value-added producers. This is exactly what economic theory would predict, of course.

The majority of forest research is conducted in the public sector, so **Hypothesis 5** is probably wrong.

There is no support for **Hypothesis 6** that industrial forestry is more likely than community forestry to conserve forests and increase carbon sequestration. Evidence from developing countries in fact (Bowler et al., 2012) indicates that community forestry increases forest density and area and hence sequestration. Evidence for increased biological diversity with community forestry is not conclusive, but the available research leans against **Hypothesis 7**.

Table 3.2: Ten possible reasons why tenure reform is not needed

Compared to a community forestry tenure system, the existing industrial forestry model will:

1. produce more wealth,
   The wealth hypothesis

2. produce more jobs,
   The employment hypothesis

3. support most people,
   The population hypothesis

4. produce most value-added,
   The value-added hypothesis

5. produce more research,
   The research hypothesis

6. achieve more carbon sequestration,
   The climate hypothesis

7. result in more forest diversity,
   The ecological hypothesis

8. generate in more secondary and tertiary economic development,
   The development hypothesis

9. create more attractive and livable communities,
   The community development hypothesis

10. produce more human capital.
    The human development hypothesis

Conclusion **37**

Hypotheses 8, 9 and **10** deal with economic, social and human development. There is simply no evidence to support the hypotheses and a variety of good arguments that suggest the hypotheses are wrong.

The startling fact is that none of these hypotheses stand up to scrutiny. The real justification of the current system is simply that it is the current system – a self-perpetuating regime of rules and institutions. It is large, old and familiar. It is supported, not by evidence, nor by theory, but by entrenched interests and the universal bias in favour of the *status quo*.

Notes

[1]Stigler argued that "every industry or occupation that has enough political power to utilize the state will seek to control entry. In addition, the regulatory policy will often be so fashioned as to retard the rate of growth of new firms." Stigler (1971)

[2]See Nelson (2008) for an excellent summary of the inadequate evidence.

Part II

ECONOMICS

4
Forests and Joint Production

Forest-based production inevitably generates linked 'products' like lumber and sawdust, oxygen and CO_2, or pulp mills and roads. In cases like this, economists speak of **joint production**.

The joint production problem is related to both externalities (see Chapter 7) and publicness (see Chapter 8), but is perhaps the most fundamental of the three. As with public goods and externalities, efficiency requires a summation of marginal costs and benefits:

$$Benefit = \sum_i B_i - C_0$$

B_i = benefits from i^{th} product
C = cost of the bundle of products

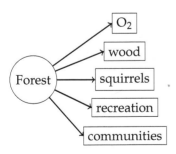

Figure 4.1: Joint products

42 Forests and Joint Production

The special feature of joint production is that costs usually depend on how much of the basic good is produced, not on the number of byproducts or whether the byproducts are sold or simply ignored. As Kant (2009) observes "forest tenures should be designed to optimize returns from all forest attributes and not only from timber."

There are fairly simple cases of joint production, as when milk as an input is turned into cheese, butter and whey. Producing cheese takes as much milk as producing cheese and whey or cheese and whey and butter. All of the end-products are owned by the same producer and have market prices. There is some room to adjust the mixture of outputs to yield, for example, more butter and less high-fat cheese, but the management problem is reasonably well understood and contained.

There are also cases of joint production that result in major social problems. When electricity is produced using coal, the inevitable joint product is CO_2. The CO_2 is usually disposed of at no cost to the firm that produces it – any effects of the CO_2 are entirely external to the firm. Baumgärtner, Faber, and Schiller (2006) argue that "joint production" of this sort is the structural cause behind modern-day environmental problems.

4.1 Joint Production in Forests

Forest companies look for ways to turn jointly produced 'byproducts' like bark or sawdust into revenue. Sawdust is now rarely burned or left to rot as it once was. Instead it maybe used as fuel, sometimes in cogeneration plants that sell electricity, or compressed to form fireplace logs. Bark is sold as garden mulch. Lignin from producing pulp may be converted to a plastic substitute used in auto bodies.

Forests also generate benefits that are not marketed and much harder for firms to internalize. They provide ecosystem goods and services, such as water storage and filtration, carbon sequestration services, and a variety of other benefits such as owl habitat, berries, mushrooms, and canoe routes. In Figure 4.2 some of the the joint products that are not appropriated by forestry companies appear

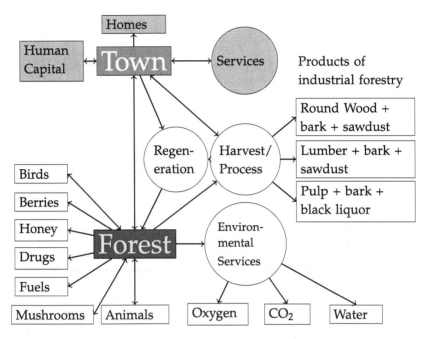

Figure 4.2: Forests as a system of joint products

on the bottom and the left. Dombeck and Moad (2001) argue that "Perhaps the most pronounced change in North American forest management over the next several decades will be a continuation of the dramatic shift in public perception concerning the value and appropriate use of forests. In particular, publicly owned natural forests will become increasingly valued for environmental services they provide – notably watershed protection, biodiversity conservation and carbon sequestration – instead of just their wood and other forest product values."

Removing wood and by-products from the system to generate revenue removes nutrients and organic material that would support animals, insects and even essential fungii. These biological 'products' may compete with others for system resources, participate in regulating the system and play essential roles in the food chain

44 *Forests and Joint Production*

Forest production also creates and supports human communities, and they in turn maintain families that produce children and, eventually, new workers. This 'social reproduction', to use the Marxist term, is not usually included in discussion of joint production, simply because it happens outside of the market system. Nonetheless, people and their capacities are always inputs to and products of forest production. They are part of the ecology of the forest. In Figure 4.2 the social products of forestry appear as shaded at the top left. The human beings and human abilities that produce and are produced by the forest community are labelled 'human capital'. 'Human capital' is a powerful metaphor, and often useful, but is also a politically contentious – it is seen by some as dangerous neoliberal propaganda. We take up the concepts of human capital and social capital in Chapter 5.

Perhaps the most profound misunderstanding of forestry is the failure to understand the ecological relationship between the forest and its human inhabitants. Forests sustain people. They support communities. People, as part of the forest community, shape the forest.

In Figure 4.2, major production processes are represented by circles. Historically governments granted rights to harvest and process, ignoring the rest of the system. As a result of a shift to 'sustainable forestry', harvest rights are coupled with responsibility for regeneration and regulations intended to protect water and some species.

4.2   *The Allocation of Rights and the Future of the Forest Community*

One way of understanding the forest tenure issue is to notice that, with conventional industrial tenure, the tenure-holder counts only values generated on the right side of Figure 4.2. Items on the lower left have no value to shareholders and the upper left, the social reproduction that is supported by the forestry industry, is actually a set of costs for the firm, not benefits. As a result, the long-run

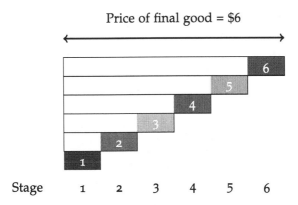

Figure 4.3: Value-added counted in six stages of production

tendency with industrial forestry is to depopulate forests. People are a cost, and efficient enterprises reduce costs. Labour-saving technological change and fossil fuel powered machinery have made it possible to greatly reduce the labour required to harvest and process trees. Given the assignment of forest rights, the system inevitably has a bias toward labour-replacing technological change. Conventional industrial forestry attempts to maintain wood exports while decreasing the burden of people. Community forestry, on the other hand, is likely to value people and to maintain community.

Is it possible to maintain or increase forest populations in the face of labour-replacing technological change? The answer to the question revolves around an understanding of value-added.

4.3 What is Value-Added?

The concept of **value-added** is essential for understanding the forestry economy. Figure 4.3 illustrates a good with six stages of production, each contributing $1 to the final price. The first stage might be cutting down a tree and delivering it to a mill. Let's follow a single board from that original tree. In the second stage the tree is cut into lumber and the lumber is dried. In stage three the our

46 *Forests and Joint Production*

board is purchased by a lumber wholesaler who sells it in a lumber yard to contractors. At stage four a contractor build a house. At stage five the house is finished and furnished. In stage six it is marketed, sold and transferred. In each stage the largest part of the value that is added is usually labour – human energy, talent and time. Forest communities mainly supply labour.

This sequence is one of the many paths that the original tree might take. The total value of transactions (all sales) in this sequence is $6 + \$5 + \$4 + \$3 + \$2 + \$1 = \$21$. Total value-added, however, is just $6, the sum of the shaded areas which represent the value-added in each stage. Usually later stages contribute larger shares. Retail markups may be 50%, effectively doubling the measured value-added on a particular good. That 50% will cover wages, rent, some profits, utilities, returns, damage, theft and so on. At the other end of the process, the wood that goes into a $1,000 coffee table may have cost the sawmill only $1.

When machines replace workers community income falls and the population of the community may decline. The value that is added by the community declines as well. If final prices stay the same, total value-added will not change but more of the value-added will go to the owners of the machines – to the shareholders and the banks.

Eventually labour-replacing technical changes reduce the total value-added. When every company has new more productive machinery, companies have to compete on prices – final prices fall, and with them, total value-added.

Mechanization and automation are continually reducing the labour content, the value that is added by communities, and the total value-added in final products. That does not imply communities should resist changes that increase productivity. Resisting leads to plant closures and declining wages. Communities that want to retain jobs and people have to find ways to add more value.

Adding value may involve making the trees more valuable through improved silvicultural practice, finding markets for additional forest products, such as mushrooms, berries or tree species not currently harvested. It could involve expanding recreational services. Tourism is just an export industry in which the customers have to pick up the product in person. Expanding value-added may involve adding more value to the lumber already produced – diverting some of the flow of wood to local manufacturing. The key point is that the long-run tendency of industrial forestry is to reduce labour inputs and the only effective response is to find ways to add value.

4.4 Valuing Ecosystem Services

The social value of the system of joint products illustrated in Figure 4.2 is

$$Benefit = \sum_i B_i - C_0,$$

where each B_i represents one of the products in the figure and the C_0 represents the costs of harvesting, processing and shipping plus any costs of ecosystem maintenance, replanting and tending the forest.

The simple formula covers a complex set of problems. What is the value of ecosystem services? What value should be used for goods when there is not market price or when the market price is not trusted?

The term *ecosystem services* was popularized by the the Millennium Ecosystem Assessment (MEA), an assessment of the effects of human activity on the environment launched in 1998 by the World Resources Institute, the United Nations Environment Programme, the World Bank and the United Nations Development Programme. More than 1,360 experts worldwide were involved in the process. It popularized the term ecosystem services and described the four classes of environmental services listed in Table 4.1: provisioning, regulating, supporting, and cultural services (World Resources Institute, 2005).

Some authors, like Spangenberg and Settele (2010), argue against trying to price ecosystem services on the grounds that "there is no such thing as an 'objective measurement' of the value of an ecosystem and its services, i.e. a measurement which (as natural scientists tend to expect) is reproducible, independent of the respective mea-

48 *Forests and Joint Production*

Table 4.1: Selected ecosystem services

Ecosystem Service	Examples
Supporting services	
soil formation	
nutrient cycling	
primary production	growth of trees
Provisioning	
food	berries, mushrooms, deer
wood and fiber	homes
fresh water	purification
fuel	
Regulating	
hydrological services	water interception and retention, flood control
climate regulation	carbon sequestration, water retention and cycling
air purification	capture of sulphur dioxide, nitrogen dioxide, dust
Cultural services	
aesthetic	
spiritual	
cultural	
recreational	

Source: Synthesis Report on Ecosystems and Human Well-Being (World Resources Institute, 2005)

surement methodology and of subjective assumptions during the measurement process" (Spangenberg and Settele, 2010). Determining the boundaries of an ecosystem depends on the question asked, and, even then, boundaries are not well defined scientifically, although they may be clear politically. Economic estimates rely on numerous assumptions, the choice of methodology, data collection methods and the availability of data. In many cases the science in not well enough developed to identify all the consequences of a proposed policy. It is not even clear what services should be evaluated. In practice what gets counted is determined through a political process that is highly sensitive to current cultural concerns and current knowledge.

Despite the real philosophical and technical difficulties described by Spangenberg and Settele, it can be useful to estimate the value of non-marketed products of the forest. At the very least the attempt is informative, and the discourse around values will help clarify what is at stake in any decision.

4.5 Valuing Non-marketed Products, Including Ecosystem Services

When all the inputs to production are purchased on the open market and all the outputs are sold it is simple to decide if a project has a positive value. Market prices are usually not available for joint products, externalities, public goods or environmental services, nor for benefits like health, accident reduction, or even education.[1]

Evaluating goods and services that do not have a market price is one of the more challenging tasks in economics. A whole collection of techniques, some of which are listed in Table 4.2, have been developed as part of the field known as cost-benefit analysis (CBA). CBA attempts to calculate money prices for for unpriced effects so that they can be taken into account in decision-making. The techniques are applied across a wide range of projects in, for example, health care, transportation, tourism and recreation, environmental resources, child care, and regulation. Each technique has its proponents and critics, and each has been the subject of a large body of research. There are variations on each technique.

In an attempt to clarify what is being measured analysts have described several categories of value that may be measured. Table 4.3 provides one classification of values. These often overlap, so it is important to be careful in combining estimates from different categories.

Different techniques are often needed for different goods and even for estimating value for different parts of the population. For example, if people are using free public parks, we might calculate time and transportation costs for various forests and use that to work out their demand function. Knowing the demand function we can estimate the net benefit they get from the park. For people who don't use the park, the value of *potential* access is an *option value*. We might use the contingent valuation approach and ask them what they would pay to retain the option. Since people often have a hard time making value estimates that reflect their actual behaviour, we might calculate a hedonic price by looking for differences in house value for neighbourhoods that have access to a park and those that do not.

Valuing the non-marketed products of a forest community can be difficult and even costly. This section is not a do-it-yourself guide: it is just a brief introduction to some of the main ideas that might be applied in managing a community forest.

4.6   Conclusions

Community forestry has the potential both to represent the public interest in a locally sensitive manner and to resolve some of the conflicts inherent in the joint product-high externality nature of forestry. In doing so it takes on some of the roles of higher level government. It may or may not involve direct production of timber or recreational services in this case, since if those activities can be assigned by government to a private producer, they can also be assigned by a community forest organization.

Conclusions **51**

Table 4.2: Valuing unpriced services

Method	Description
Hedonic pricing	Extracting implicit prices for components of a package of experiences, for example, calculating the value of access to lake from the amounts people pay for cottages close to and far from a lake.
Travel cost method	(Clawson method) A revealed preference method that uses travel cost data to calculate how much people value national parks, beaches, ecosystems, etc.
Contingent valuation	A survey-based method for eliciting values by asking questions like "How much would you pay for an increase in ....?" Sometimes called the 'stated preference' method in contrast to the 'revealed preference' method.
Choice Modelling	A preference approach in which respondents rank or rate descriptions of goods. Descriptions may include price. As with hedonic pricing, regression is used to extract implicit prices.
Conjoint analysis	A regression approach to extracting information from a series of questions of the form "Which of these do you prefer?"
MLE-CLR	(Maximum likelihood estimation by censored logistic regression) A statistical approach to analyzing 'referendum data' arising from questions of the form, "Would you pay $100 to have this highway built: yes or no?"
Production function methods	Estimates production functions and uses marginal productivity to value resources created, protected or lost.
Damage cost avoided	Calculates cost avoided as a result of a project.
Adjusted market prices	Corrects prices for externalities, subsidies, taxes and other distortions.

52 *Forests and Joint Production*

Table 4.3: Market and non-market values

Value Type	Description
Market value	The exchange value or price of a commodity in the open market.
Intrinsic value	The value of entities that may have little or no market value, but have use value.
Intrinsic non-use value	The value attached to the environment and life forms for their own sake.
Existence value	The value attached to the knowledge that species, natural environments and other ecosystem services exist, even if the individual does not contemplate ever making active use of them.
Bequest and vicarious values	A willingness to pay to preserve the environment for the benefit of other people, intra and intergenerationally.
Present value	The value today of a future asset, discounted to the present.
Option value	A willingness to pay a certain sum today for the future use of an asset.
Quasi-option value	The value of preserving options for future use assuming an expectation of increasing knowledge about the functioning of the natural environment.

Based on Kumar and Kumar (2008) p. 809, as adapted from Gilpin (2000).

Notes

[1] Values may be changing over time as well. In "Conservation Reconsidered," John Krutilla (1967) highlighted a new focus in resource economics. Krutilla made a compelling argument that technology is much better able to provide substitutes for resource commodities than for resource amenities; as a result, the relative value of resource amenities should be expected to increase over time.

5

Human Capital and Social Capital

In its simplest sense, capital is simply an accumulation of wealth (Richards, 1926).[1] Capital is more than just wealth, however: it is *productive* wealth. The distinction is caught rather neatly in the sentiment first expressed by the writer Anne Isabella Richie, in a story in the 1880s:

> "Give a man a fish and you feed him for a day. Teach a man to fish and you feed him for a lifetime".[2]

A fish is a form of consumable wealth. A pond stocked with fish, a fishing pole, and the skill to use it are three kinds of productive capital that together produce a lifelong stream of wealth (at least in the story).

The modern sense of the the word capital has developed from a 17th-century term for the funds that partners put up to advance a project. Postlethwayt's 1751 *Universal Dictionary of Trade and Commerce* gives us this:[3]

> "CAPITAL, amongst merchants, bankers, and traders, signifies the sum of money which individuals bring to make up the common stock of a partnership when it is first formed. It is also said of the stock which a merchant at first puts into trade, for his account".

Capitalism, of course, is the system in which this type of financial investment is the driving force of the economy. Money capital is invested today in order to produce more money capital in the future.

Over time the term 'capital' came to be applied to any asset acquired by the capitalist enterprise to provide a financial return. Economists came to use the term 'real capital', to mean the entire physical stock of goods and machinery that the 'owners of capital' combine with labour and land. In Figure 5.1 'real' capital appears as 'produced capital'. The broad, modern sense of 'capital' evolves from this emphasis on the real, productive, physical capital.[4]

The essential features of "real capital"

- Capital takes time and energy to create in the present (requires *investment*)
- Capital produces a stream of benefits (is *productive*)
- Capital lasts a long time (is *durable*)
- Capital wears out with use (it *depreciates*)
- Capital relates present costs to future benefits and, in its original commercial sense,
- Capital can be owned, bought and sold, or transferred (is *property*)

5.1 Modern Extensions of the Concept of Capital

The concept of capital has been extended in ways that would certainly have surprised and possibly have delighted those (Richards, 1926) who originally popularized the word in English. A.C. Pigou (1928) may have launched the formal capital-theoretic approach to human abilities in the modern neoclassical economic literature when he wrote "There is such a thing as investment in human capital as well as investment in material capital". The approach took off with "Investment in Human Capital and Personal Income Distribution" by

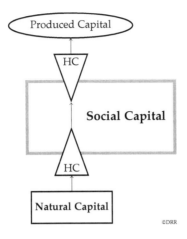

Figure 5.1: A simple material culture

Jacob Mincer (1958) in the Journal of Political Economy and became a field of study in its own right with *Human Capital: A Theoretical and Empirical Analysis, with Special Reference to Edcuation* by Nobel Memorial prize-winner Becker (1964). There is also a long but largely informal use of the term social capital going back to Hanifan (1916) and extending through Jane Jacobs (1961). The concept surfaced in political science with Salisbury (1969) and came into wide use by the 1990s with, for example, Robert Putnam (2000) and *Bowling Alone*. There is now a large literature on social capital and there is no need to review it here – the fundamental point is that the extension of this fundamentally economic concept is relatively recent. It is of some interest that much of the work has been done outside of the economics profession.

Precisely because the concept of capital has been so widely applied, so frequently re-invented and, unfortunately, so often abused, it is helpful to start with an account of capital in a simplified society. Figure 5.1 presents relationships among four types of capital in a simple material culture. At this stage, human society has developed a culture (social capital) that it reproduces through the generations. Individuals and groups gather materials from the natural world and

58 *Human Capital and Social Capital*

either consume those materials or produce goods that last from period to period. These lasting products – tools, pots, weapons, homes, clothing – are the "materials" of the material culture.

In the parable at the beginning of the chapter, the pond stocked with fish is natural capital, the fishing rod is produced capital and the skill to use the fishing rod is human capital. Who does the teaching? The knowledge about how to fish and the ability to pass that knowledge on are social capital, achievements of the whole society. Unmentioned in the parable, someone with human capital was using social knowledge to produce the fishing rod. The society in Figure 5.1 is pre-capitalist. Calling the various elements "capitals" in this case is a bit like calling the fins of a fish "feet" just because, some millions of years later and on a very different species, the analogous appendage will be called feet. In modern terms, capital is first and foremost a property relation. The elements called capital in Figure 5.1 are human capacities, social capacities and natural or produced usefulness.

5.2   Types of Capital

Economists identify at least five major types of capital: natural capital, social capital, human capital, produced capital and financial capital. Within each there are sub-types. Natural capital, for example, includes land, minerals, fish, the atmosphere, and ecological systems. Social capital includes morals and financial systems, trust and social networks. Natural capital forms the base for all the others. Human skills are needed to make a living from nature. Other skills can produce tools, homes, roads and bridges. The human capital is created[5] out of culture, the basic form of social capital that includes language and the accumulated knowledge of the community. Institutions, including the family, resting on habit, social norms, mythologies, law, and even force, reproduce the human capacities and regulate human activities.

5.2.1 Industrial, Financial and Commercial Capital

One special form of social capital is credit, with the credit markets and all the supporting institutions that help to allocate capital and time. Financial capital is a special form of credit owned by individuals and historically used to 'finance' project and enterprises. Financial capital is a new social institution that changes the way production is regulated and defines modern society. Figure 5.2 illustrates what happens when we add finance capital to the simple model.

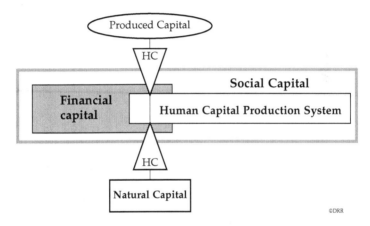

Figure 5.2: A modern capitalist culture

In Figure 5.2, financial or money capital hires the labour, purchases the resources and the machinery, and determines what is produced. As a result very little market production can occur without the participation of financial capital, and financial capital can extract profits from the process. The profits are added to the pool of financial capital, which must then be reinvested.

Financial capital is not in itself productive: it works by controlling other forms of capital. Financial capital is essentially just ownership of the product of other forms of capital. Financial capital is always growing, and to grow it constantly pushes to extend its ownership over natural, social and even human capital. That is what is happening when corporations lobby for expanded intellectual property

60 *Human Capital and Social Capital*

rights, patent genes, privatize education, and lend money to governments or even students.

5.2.2 *Natural Capital*

Land was one of the three *factors of production* recognized by Classical economists. It was a "gift of nature" that was owned by a specific social class – the "landowners" – and it provided them with a steady income that came to be called "rent". Land is now understood as just one kind of *natural capital.*

Other forms include renewable resources like trees and fish stocks as well as non-renewable resources like ore bodies and natural systems like steams, lakes and forests. 'Natural capital' is a metaphor, and extension of the concept of capital, but it is also a central concept for understanding a resource-based economy. The main assets in many regions are varieties of natural resource. Clean air and fresh water are among the "environmental services" that flow from natural capital.

Nature and its services only become 'capital' when they are owned by capitalists. In a funny way, capital absorbs and renames nature – as it does with anything else that can be made into a tradable asset.

5.3 *Human Capital*

Human capital is a term applied to human abilities, whether they are innate talents or the result of education. If the abilities are produced by education, then the cost of education can be seen as an investment that yields a productive asset. The asset is 'capital' because it has the properties of produced capital described above: it takes time and energy to create, produces a stream of benefits, is durable, and depreciates.

The term 'human capital' is a useful metaphor for thinking about education. It also subtly redefines each person as a capitalist investing in a productive asset that can be sold on the labour market.

It suggests that every single person is logically equivalent to the owners of financial capital, who, technically, are the capitalists. It encourages us to consider education in general as primarily preparing labour commodities for the market. Critics believe that using the term 'human capital' amounts to collaborating with the 'neoliberal agenda',[6] which is to bring every aspect of society and life under market control.

The criticisms are legitimate but the metaphor is still useful. Student debt, for example, represents a promise to pay the lender some part of the student's future wages. From the point of view of the lender it is an investment that gives the lender ownership of the product of the human capital supposedly created through education. Slavery itself is illegal in modern societies, but student debt, like other kinds of consumer debt, slips past the legal definition, making the student a capital asset that is is a sense 'owned' by financial capital.

In a general sense all economic activity is about producing and reproducing people. The fact that communities fund schools indicates that creating human beings with useful capacities is seen as an essential social activity, (and possibly as one too important to entrust to the private sector). In community forestry, human capital itself should be understood as one of the most important products. Human capital is not an incidental product of forest communities – it is the primary product.

For private producers however, human capital is an incidental joint product for which they are not paid.[7] The reason for the perceived shortage of skilled trades in some advanced countries is simply that employers are reluctant to invest in skill development because they cannot reliably capture the return on skills developed. Forestry companies with conventional tenure might have some interest in producing human capital, but their interest is obviously less direct than the interest of the community as a whole. Responsibility for human capital formation has therefore increasingly fallen to the public sector.

62 Human Capital and Social Capital

5.3.1 Community Forestry and the Production of Human Capital

Communities, on the other hand, have historically been responsible for local education, and families in a community have a direct stake in effective education. A community forestry organization would be more likely than a large firm to look for ways to combine forestry operations and local education, hoping to improve both. It might, for example, encourage the study of silviculture in the local schools, employ local students in operations, support schools in doing silvicultural research, and accept the responsibility for supervising apprenticeships. Alfred Gamble (forthcoming) describes the Beardy's and Okemasis First Nation in Saskatchewan doing exactly this kind of human capital development. Furthermore, since community forest organizations are easily seen as representatives of the public interest with respect to these issues, and forest companies can rarely make this claim, community forestry organizations should be freer to experiment with this kind of integration than purely commercial operators.

A plausible goal in economic development is the expansion of human capacities and freedoms.[8] These are supported by a complex of accumulated assets – physical, social and human capitals. Understanding development therefore requires an understanding of the nature of, accumulation of, and distribution of these capitals. The notion of sustainable development also requires a precise understanding of different kinds of capital.

5.3.2 Social Capital

Like natural capital and human capital, the concept of social capital is a metaphorical extension of the term capital. There are two common conceptions of social capital, a sociological approach designed for the analysis of power and privilege, and economic approach that emphasizes structures that make the community more productive.

A sociological emphasis on stratification, class, privilege and power naturally leads to theorizing social capital as a private asset from which some are excluded. The concept of social capital as an individual acquisition is associated with Bourdieu (1986). According to Partha Dasgupta (2003), however, social capital should not be defined in terms of what it delivers; rather, it should be regarded directly as social structure. "If the externalities ... are 'confined', social capital is an aspect of 'human capital', in the sense economists use the latter term". Bourdieu's social capital is just private human capital for Dasgupta.[9]

In economic theory, social capital is usually treated as a public or a local public good. The focus is on the productivity of the social asset and the costs of producing it: James Coleman (1990) (who served as president of the American Sociological Association, incidentally), gave an essentially economic interpretation. In *The Foundations of Social Theory* he defines social capital in terms of productivity: it is

> social organization .... facilitating the achievement of goals that could not be achieved in its absence or could be achieved only at a higher cost (p 304)

Similarly, Putnam, Leonardi, and Nanetti (1993) also treat social capital as collective assets:

> social capital ... refers to features of social organization, such as trust, norms, and *networks* (our emphasis) that can improve the efficiency of society... (p. 167) [10]

According to Dasgupta (2003), "social capital is most usefully viewed as a system of interpersonal networks". This is the approach employed by the OECD[11] and used in Chapter 10 to explore the innovation potential of community forestry.

Social capital includes the networks that make it possible for people to work together and solve problems efficiently. It includes trust and respect for the law, deeply set attitudes that reduce the cost of transactions and improve the quality of life. More broadly social capital also includes the professional organizations that collect and pass on their specialized knowledges, the system of institutions and teachers, the skills of the police force and even the manners of store clerks. The entire financial system that provides credit and helps to allocate investment is also a form of social capital.

64 *Human Capital and Social Capital*

Social capital differs from the traditional economic notion of capital: it isn't owned by individuals, it is a public good that provides benefits to all the members of a group that possesses it. Instead of wearing out when it is used, social capital often grows (Ostrom, 2000).

The World Bank increasingly emphasizes the importance of social capital on development and "social capital research increasingly informs the design and evaluation of World Bank-supported projects and policies" (Dudwick et al., 2006). The Bank has developed qualitative and quantitative tools for measuring social capital.

5.4 Community Forestry, Development and Social Capital

The role of community forestry in economic and social development has received considerable attention. Sunderlin, Hatcher, and Liddle (2008), for example, considers the role of community forestry in the alleviation of poverty. Bray et al. (2003, 2006) apply concepts from common property theory and social and natural capital to analyze the emergence and operation of "a very large sector of community forests managed for the commercial production of timber".

Concern for human development provides one answer to a question raised by Luckert (1999). Why bother maintaining forestry communities that developed to serve an industrial mode that no longer needs them? The answer is not that the communities in some sense deserve special exemption from the forces of the market. A sentimental concern for a dying way of life may be a poor guide to forest policy, as Luckert points out. A more convincing argument rests on the value of these communities to the rest of society. Forest-based communities can be a place where human talents are developed while providing indispensable environmental and economic services.

Any community engaged in production creates considerable social capital. Community organizations invest in public works, develop schools, and support sports organizations. They will have opportunities to provide members of the community with connections and practice in working with others that expand individual's social capacity, and they will have strong incentives to improve the communal institutions and networks. These investments provide little or no return to the owners of a conventional forestry firm. Economic theory therefore predicts that under the current tenure regime there will be under-investment in social capital for forest communities.

Furthermore, climate change, carbon sequestration programmes and rising wood values are likely to require enhanced levels of forest stewardship. The people in these communities would then have an expanded role in caring for the forests of their regions. The interests of the forest communities are already intrinsically aligned, not with current social policy, but with a more ambitious and forward-looking forestry policy (such as those courses of policy outlined by Palmer and Smith (forthcoming)). They just need the social policy to catch up.

Experts believe that adding value to wood is the only possible direction for increasing employment and wealth in forest-based regions (Moazzami, 2006). If Crown forest tenure systems around the world are reformed to encourage the development of value-added forestry – both pre- and post-harvest – then forest-based communities will be the basis of wealth creation that benefits the larger society.

Notes

[1] Generically "capital" stands for a stock of produced or natural factors of production that can be expected to yield productive services for some time. (Solo (2000))

[2] The modern form used here dates from the 1960s, when it began to be called an 'ancient Chinese proverb'.

[3] From "Early History of the Term Capital," by Edwin Cannan, *Quarterly Journal of Economics*, volume 35 (1921).

[4] Capital is a **stock** quantity, as opposed to a **flow**. Water in a tub is a stock, water flowing out is a flow. A flow quantity has a time interval as a part of its measure, for example litres per minute or tons per year. A stock variable has no interval, as in gallons in the tank, or vehicles in an inventory.

[5] "It is in fact impossible to account for the structure and functioning of the social world unless one reintroduces capital in all its forms and not solely in the one form recognized by economic theory". (Bourdieu, 1986)

[6] Neoliberalism a set of ideas and policies associated with the theories of economists Friedrich Hayek and Milton Friedman. Central is a commitment to relying on market solutions and minimizing government.

[7] As early as 1912 A.C Pigou observed that industry will not invest enough in training workers for the simple reason that they cannot reliably get their investment back.

[8] The concept here is loosely that of Amartya Sen, which is now embodied in the Human Development Index.

[9] Bourdieau's notion of the return to social capital is analogous to the rents that a landlord collects from possessing a particularly desirable piece of land.

[10] Cited in Durlauf and Fafchamps (2004).

[11] "Rather than invent a new definition, it has been agreed that the OECD definition be adopted for use across UK government departments. The definition is as follows: 'networks together with shared norms, values and understandings that facilitate cooperation within or among groups'." Cote and Healy (2001), p. 41.

6
The Efficiency of Community Forestry

The most important efficiency result in economic theory – and almost certainly the most important theorem in all of the social sciences – is the First Fundamental Theorem of Welfare Economics. This theorem states that, under certain circumstances market-determined prices will result in an allocation of resources that is 'nice' in a specific, somewhat limited but very important sense.

It is a proposition that goes back at least to 1776 and Adam Smith's then unproven "invisible hand" hypothesis; that competitive markets tend toward an efficient allocation of resources.[1] The proposition was refined by a long series of economists including Harold Hotelling and Abba P. Lerner and was rigorously proven by Arrow (1951)

The First Theorem is enormously important politically. Because it says that markets can be efficient, it is often taken as a justification for relying on markets for almost every allocation problem. With the First Theorem lurking in the background of any economic discussion, the view that that forestry is a competitive industry seems to support the assumption that the existing forestry system is more or less efficient, and that any public action aimed at changing the system would lead to inefficiency.

In this chapter I will show that, at least in theory, community forestry is more efficient than the industrial tenure system that dominates countries such as Canada. The argument is "theoretical".

although not particularly difficult. I will discuss what economists mean by efficiency, what the First Theorem tells us and what it doesn't tell us. Then I will present two propositions that might be called the "Fundamental Theorems of Community Forestry".

6.1 Pareto Efficiency

Efficiency is a fairly simple concept: *if it is not possible to do better with a given collection of resources, then the resources are being used efficiently.* Defining "better" and "given resources" is the tricky part. It turns out that the superiority of community forestry turns on a re-examination of both concepts.

Lets start with 'better'. People may not agree that one outcome is better than another. How do we resolve the problem? One approach is to only consider changes that everyone can agree to.

Figure 6.1: Portrait of Vilfredo Pareto (1848–1923)

The problem can be seen at its simplest if we imagine a situation with just two people on a sinking ship and a lifeboat with just one seat remaining. One will live and one will die (or, if you can't make a decision, both will die). How do you decide which one should be saved?

There are two equally unattractive solutions. Choosing is really impossible unless you have a theory that tells you why one person is more valuable than the other, and economists don't pretend to have any such theory.

Say, though, one person is already in the lifeboat. This can be seen as a very different problem. Now one of them is in *possession* of a seat in the lifeboat. In order to give the seat to the other you have to take it away from the one in possession.

Pareto Efficiency **69**

You might want to question how the first came to possess the seat, and you might question whether simply arriving first is a sufficient justification for possession. If, however, you accept possession as a starting point, the problem goes away.

In this case you cannot make the person without a seat better off without making the person with the seat worse off. Economists say the situation is "Pareto Efficient". A Pareto *improvement* is a change that makes at least one person better off while making no one worse off.

Restricting ourselves to Pareto improvements narrows down the alternatives that we can consider. It actually limits changes to arrangements that everyone agrees to, since anyone can veto a solution that makes him worse off. Restricting ourselves to Pareto improvements rules out taking a dollar from a billionaire to save the life of a child.

It is possible that the person with the seat might want to give it up. An adult might voluntarily give a lifeboat seat to a child. A billionaire might gladly donate a dollar. These would be Pareto improvements because the possessor agrees that the resulting allocation is better. It is possible that the person without the seat might 'buy' the seat with a promise. This would also be a Pareto improvement.

The First Fundamental Theorem of Welfare Economics states that under certain circumstances market-determined prices will result in an allocation that is Pareto efficient. It is a remarkable result, but perhaps not entirely mysterious when we realize that all the transactions in the market are voluntary, and that no one is supposed to accept a trade that makes them worse off. Each change in the market then must result in a Pareto improvement, and trading should not stop until there are no more Pareto improvements to be had. At that point the allocations must be Pareto efficient.

The proofs of the First Theorem by Arrow and Debreu rely on a number of reasonably strong assumptions, including: very large numbers of buyers; the absence of externalities; perfectly rational sellers; and perfect information. The conditions required for the theorem's proof are unlikely to hold in the real world, but they are

70 *The Efficiency of Community Forestry*

only sufficient conditions – not necessary conditions. It is possible to have Pareto efficient markets even if the conditions used in the proof are not satisfied.

It seems likely that many markets do achieve something sufficiently close to Pareto efficiency and that some markets require government interventions to achieve satisfactory results. We will argue that externalities are ubiquitous in forest production, and that, as a result, it is unlikely that the current arrangements are efficient.

Pareto efficiency is a fairly limited goal. It does not take account of notions of fairness or human development, and it restricts the set of permissible changes to those that no one would veto given their initial allocation. It essentially takes the initial allocation of property and rights as sacred. A society in which one person owns everything could be Pareto efficient.

6.2   *Welfarist Notions of Efficiency*

There is a less restrictive way to think about efficiency that we want to use in this chapter. Imagine a mother with several children and a bag of toffees. She might give one to the smallest child, two to each of her middle children and none to the oldest. She might be sure that this is going to produce the greatest happiness because she knows exactly how much pleasure the children would get from the candies.

There are fairness issues to deal with in a case like this, but if mother knows the children's true preferences and what is good for them, she can allocate the candies in a way that maximizes the happiness of her family. In other words, she can find an efficient allocation. No initial allocation of wealth restricts her decisions. This is the basic principle in the 'welfarist' approach. For many purposes economists want to know about how we would allocate resources if we knew people's preferences perfectly.

Of course we don't know people's preferences and we have no reliable way to comparing the happiness of one person the the happiness of another. We can't really maximize what we can't measure. Nonetheless, there is a good deal to be learned from acting as if we can measure individual welfare (or utility, or happiness). Every economist is taught how to set up the welfare maximization problem and derive the conditions that describe the most efficient allocation. In many cases the resulting "marginal conditions" can be used as guidelines even without knowing people's actual preferences.

For example, we can show that it is better that everyone face the same prices, that the marginal cost of producing the last unit of soup should be equal to the price the producer gets, that monopolies make a community poorer, that most subsidies are not welfare improving, and that taxes on different goods should generally be equal in a special sense. The list of conditions that must be true at a welfare maximum is extensive and it provides valuable guidance for policy-makers.

The mathematics of welfare maximization is very simple in principle. On the one hand we have a mathematical function that does a reasonable job of representing what you want. The function is called an 'objective function': our objective is to find the settings for any variables we control that will give us the the highest possible value of this function. The objective can be profits, utility, happiness, energy – mathematically it doesn't matter. There are some mathematical conditions that must be true when we have achieved the highest value of the objective function, and they can tell us interesting things about the solution. In our case we are interested in 'social welfare', which is a function that somehow adds up the satisfaction of everyone in the community, as mother does in the example above.

We argue that community forestry can be more efficient than conventional industrial forestry because it is more likely to be maximizing the right social welfare function. In other words, community forestry may employ a better definition of 'better'.

On the other side of the problem we have one of more functions that limit our choices. These last are called 'constraints'. The constraints divide the set of actions into ones that are possible (allowed, or feasible) and ones that are not. The constraints could arise, for example, because of the limitations of the available technology, regulations, or limits on the availability of supplies, The trick is to make

72 *The Efficiency of Community Forestry*

choices that yield the highest value for the objective function from the set of possible actions.

The argument made below is that community forestry can be more efficient than conventional industrial forestry because some some constraints are likely to be relaxed. With more permissible choices a community forestry organization may be able to achieve a higher value for the objective function.

6.3 *What Can a Community Do?*

Let's start by considering what happens if a constraint is relaxed. The easiest case is when a producer is not allowed to change some variables that would affect its profits.[2] The variables could represent permissible emissions, or the speed limit on local roads, the hours of work, the use of child labour, the amount of arsenic in milk, or the kind of equipment used. Firms are always subject to restrictions like this.

In this case we assume that a forestry company can control a list of variables that we will call x. These include employment decisions, investment decisions, times of operation, and so on.

A basic result in economic theory states that relaxing a constraint can't hurt.[3] In common language, you can do more with a hammer and a saw than you can with just a hammer.

The principle can be expressed mathematically this way. Say Π is whatever you want to maximize and that both x and y can influence the value of Π. For now lets assume that Π stands for profit. We can say with confidence that

$$\max_{x,y} \Pi \geq \max_{x} \Pi, \tag{6.1}$$

The inequality says that if you control both x and y, you can't do worse than if you only control x. The logic is simple enough: it is always possible to not use an extra tool, so it is always possible to do as well as you would if you didn't have the tool. Since you will only use the tool if it makes you better off, you can't be worse off and will generally be better off with more tools.

A community forestry organization is essentially a type of local government. As a representative of the public interest a community forestry organization can legitimately influence some variables that are not entrusted to private operators.

This is a fundamental observation about the nature of community forestry: the community would control the same set of variables as a forestry company, but it would also control some variables that are not under the control of the forestry company. It yields a basic result about the economics of community forestry.

> **The First Fundamental Property of Community Forestry:**
> A community forest operation will be able to generate at least as much **profit** as a private forestry company can achieve if the community forestry has control of additional variables because of its status as a community organization.

With all the tools available to a private firm, a community forestry operation could simply imitate the way a private firm would behave and achieve the same outcome as a private firm. Alternatively, it could sublet its tenure to a private firm with the normal restrictions that the firm would normally operate under. The tenant firm would then make exactly the same decision as it would have if the community forestry organization did not have the additional freedoms.

6.4 What Does a Community Want?

The second fundamental observation about community forestry is that a community has a broader stake in the management of its forest than a private firm will have. The community might be concerned about water quality, attracting tourists, training the local young people, minimizing road repair, property tax revenues, harvesting non-timber forest products and creating new businesses. These are all legitimate economic concerns, but they are not included in the profits of a private firm.

74 *The Efficiency of Community Forestry*

Clearly if a forestry company values only profits $(p \cdot x)$ it will not automatically take care of the environment, nor will it maximize local job creation or invest in more than the minimum of human and social capital. The company may generate a negative externality through emissions or by generating noise. It will not be concerned to protect jobs or achieve other social objectives because these are not included in the firm's objective function. Shareholders' experience of the company is essentially summarized by profits, and management is expected to maximize profit, not some other expression that represents the public interest.

We can express the economic problem for a forestry company in the following way: *Maximize profits given the features of the forest, the labour market, the technology available and subject to any enforceable rules.* Using a shorthand notation we can write

$$\max_{x} \Pi = p \cdot x \tag{6.2}$$

$$subject\ to$$

$$T(x,y,z) = 0,$$

$$R(x,y,z) = 0,$$

where Π stands for the company's profits, x stands for everything the company buys – including labour, machinery, power vehicles, insurance licences and supplies – or sells – which would include any products of the operations. p is just the list of prices, including various wages. For purchases the price is negative. The expression $p \cdot x$ is just a very short way to write revenue minus expenditure.

The expression $T(x,y,z) = 0$ stands for any technological limitations. It might specify how much labour, how many trucks, how much roadbuilding and so on is required to harvest a given quantity of salable timber of a given type in each section of the SFL. Similarly, $R(x,y,z) = 0$ specifies any rules or regulations that apply. One part of R might specify that for every tree of type A that is cut, 10 seedlings must be planted. Costly effort can even be allocated to changing the rules. The details are not important for this discussion.

If the executive council of the community forestry organization were only interested in profits we could express the economic problem the following way: *Maximize profits given the features of the forest, the labour market, the technology available and subject to any enforceable rules.*

Since the community controls variables that are not available to the forestry company we can write

$$\max_{x,\,\mathbf{y}} \Pi = p \cdot x \qquad (6.3)$$

subject to

$$T(x, \mathbf{y}, z) = 0,$$
$$R(x, \mathbf{y}, z) = 0$$

The difference is the addition of the extra control variables y. In this formulation the managers of the community forest can manipulate the rules or even the technology to make the company more profitable. If we allow some of the ys to stand for prices, the community forest could increase profit by buying some unpriced output. It might, for example, pay the company to supply garbage services, allowing the firm to achieve some economies of scale while cutting costs for the community.[4]

However, If the executive council of the community forestry organization were concerned about more than just profits it would want to maximize a broader measure of social welfare, say W. This objective function might include variables like air quality, opportunities for young people, and, say, municipal costs. Let's call this collection of variables z. Furthermore, let's assume that the organization knows the value, v, of all the elements in z and exactly how a change in andy x will affect z.

The goal is now to *maximize **benefits to the whole community** given the features of the forest, the labour market, the technology available and subject to any enforceable rules.* This can be written as follows:

76 *The Efficiency of Community Forestry*

$$\max_{x} W = p \cdot x + \mathbf{v} \cdot \mathbf{z} \qquad (6.4)$$

$$subject\ to$$

$$T(x, y, \mathbf{z}) = 0,$$

$$R(x, y, \mathbf{z}) = 0$$

We are making a couple assumptions about the **capacity** of the executive council at this point. It has to be able to value the additional variables, so let's assume that the accountant for the council[5] can come up with measures of air quality, opportunities and the impact on the municipal budget (z), and furthermore can deduce reasonable prices, v, for air quality, opportunities and the impact on the municipal budget. Estimating these values is the task of cost-benefit analysis.

To get the next proposition in the simplest mathematical form it is convenient to introduce an odd little expression: Let x^{Π} be the value of x that maximizes profit (Π) without considering any effect on z. This is the x that the company would choose in Equation 6.2. The term

$$x^{\Pi} = (argmax\ \Pi) \qquad (6.5)$$

should be read "the value of the argument x that maximizes profit (Π) when only x is controlled".

Similarly x^{W} and y^{W} are the values of x and y that maximize W. These are the values of x and y that would be chosen by the community forest managers on behalf of the community in Equation 6.4. We can write

$$W(x^{W}) \geq W(x^{\Pi}) \qquad (6.6)$$

This simply states the obvious: a company trying to maximize profits will not generally achieve as much community welfare, W, as a community that is trying to maximize welfare, and it will probably do worse.[6]

Conclusions **77**

The Second Fundamental Property of Community Forestry:
A community forest operation will achieve the goals of the community
more reliably than a private forestry company if the community is
interested in more than profits for stockholders.

The proposition depends on the implicit assumption that the
community can hire talent, mobilize capital, and ensure ethical
behaviour roughly as easily as a conventional firm. It says nothing
about the adjustment period that might be required to develop
the institutional forms and the human capital to handle the more
complex problem that maximizing W involves.

6.5 Conclusions

In debates over tenure reform it has been argued that Community
forestry is economically inferior to large-scale industrial forestry,
although it is generally thought to be more equitable and environmentally sounder. The analysis presented here suggests, on the
contrary, that community forestry would be economically superior to
industrial forestry and would deliver benefits that industrial forestry
cannot. The benefits of conventional tenure are available within a
community forestry framework. The converse is not true: many of
the benefits of community forestry are not available under conventional forest tenure. An implication is that **community forestry is a
more general form than conventional industrial tenures**.

The Third Fundamental Property of Community Forestry:
Community forestry is a more general form than conventional industrial tenures in the sense that the results of conventional industrial
tenure may be achieved by **restricting** the powers and the concerns of
a community forestry organization.

The economic advantage of community forestry arises in part
because community control can achieve **economies of scope** without
giving up the **economies of scale**. Economies of scope arise when
costs can be spread over a larger *range* of outputs. Producing two

78 *The Efficiency of Community Forestry*

lines of chairs may be only a little more expensive than producing one. *Economies of scale*, which are the principal advantage of conventional industrial forestry, arise when costs can be spread over a larger *quantity* of output. Buying a second sawmill and eliminating of one of the accounting departments reduces average cost. Economies of scope may also arise because of opportunities to value outcomes or products that cannot be monetized by privately held forest firms and to mobilize resources that cannot be mobilized by firms. Furthermore, community forest organizations can be given broad decision-making powers because they are easily seen as representatives of the public interest with respect to many issues, making it possible to achieve certain economies. Forest companies can rarely claim to be representative of the public interest.[7]

We can summarize the theoretical argument in terms of the two terms introduced above – "y" standing for additional variables that the community forest can control, and "z" standing for additional concerns of the community forest – that capture the ways that community forestry expands the choices available. Any comparison of community forestry and the current regime that fails to specify these adequately is simply not valid. It will have misunderstood the economic nature of community forestry.

Notes

[1] Adam Smith, *An Inquiry into the Nature and Causes of the Wealth of Nations* (1776). London: W. Strahan. See a facsimile on Google books.

[2] Allowing tenure holders to make free choices with respect to product mix, inputs mix, choices of technology, the allocation of capital and markets they choose to serve will increase efficiency and help improve competitiveness. Vertinsky and Luckert (2010)

[3] It is possible to come up with cases where having more choices might lead to bad outcomes. In general such examples depend on ignorance, wilful stupidity, jealousy or externalities. The exceptions are entertaining but irrelevant for this discussion.

[4] In principle a community might pay a forestry company that it didn't own, but transaction and monitoring costs would probably be higher, liability questions would be harder to solve and effort would be spent in rent-seeking. Although communities and companies often assist each other, theory suggests that many opportunities will be passed over. A lot of "small change" will be left on the table.

[5] The collection of techniques for calculating and comparing benefits and costs of a project taking into account unmeasured variables and variables that may not have a market price is known as Cost Benefit Analysis (CBA). The organization would need an accountant familiar with CBA.

[6] Obviously it is also true that

$$W(x^W, y^W) \geq\geq W(x^{\Pi})$$

[7] The conventional forestry industry may recognize the potential advantages of community forestry. The Ontario Forest Industry Association, an industry organization that defended the existing tenure regime, issued a statement during consultation of tenure in Ontario that essentially argued y should not be permitted and z should not be considered in evaluation community forestry experiments.

7
Externalities and Community Forestry

The idea of external costs and benefits is one of the very important contributions economics makes to policy analysis. The concept has wide application in forestry management.

At its root, the concept is really political: it is based on noticing who counts and who doesn't for the person making decisions. The people who count are 'insiders'. Everyone else is an outsider. You can think of insiders as living in a gated community. If they dump garbage over the wall, the garbage is gone as far as they are concerned. For firms, shareholders are inside the box and non-shareholders are outsiders. Profit maximizing firms don't care much about what happens "outside of the box".

A cost that falls on someone other than the decision-maker is called an **externality**. The cost of pollution resulting from production is generally 'external' to the firm. When private producers are not charged for negative externalities, they will ignore the effects and will "oversupply" the pollution. In the same way, when consumers are not charged for CO_2 emissions they will "oversupply" CO_2.

The resulting level of output is usually not efficient. In the economics literature, when a market fails to achieve efficiency it is known as a **market failure**. For markets to produce efficient results, external costs and benefits must be fully counted by the decision-

82 *Externalities and Community Forestry*

makers. A policy or process that makes decision-makers take external effects into account is said to "internalize" the cost.

7.1 *Calculations for a Global Catastrophe*

Burning coal to produce electricity generates an external cost when the carbon dioxide warms the climate. Neither producers nor consumers consider this cost. Stockholders get 100% of the profits they earn from selling the electricity. Consumers get 100% of the benefit from the electricity they purchase. Unfortunately, they both share the cost of global warming with the other seven billion people on the globe. Their share of the cost is so small that they ignore it.

To see how powerful the effect is, consider a simple case. Say a power company makes just $1 from selling the power from a ton of coal. If there are 100,000 shares in the company, shareholders get 1/1000 of a penny.

A common (but low) estimate of the cost to the world of releasing a ton of CO_2 is $70.00. Since the cost is spread over about 7 billion people, each person, and each shareholder, suffers by one one-millionth of a cent for each ton burned.

Shareholders are not likely to worry about the total external effect even though it is 70 times larger than the benefit they receive as shareholders. As insiders, the benefit of burning coal is a thousand times larger than their share of the cost.

There are also positive externalities. Painting your house or fixing up your garden adds to the market value of other homes on your street. A successful society develops ways to encourage acts that generate positive externalities.

7.2   Externalities and Community Forestry

The concept of an externality has wide application in community forestry. If, for example, the timber harvest affects water quality downstream, the harvester will usually ignore those costs because they are borne by others. That is why forestry legislation includes rules designed to protect watersheds. The members of a community forestry organization will usually live in the watershed where they harvest. Their own water supply may be affected. As a result, they are more likely to protect water quality than a private forestry company would be. Many externalities for the firm can be 'internalized" in the move to community forestry.

It can be useful to think of 'ecosystem services' as a positive externality generated by forests. The entire world may benefit from the carbon storage and air purification provided by the forest. The local community, company and government benefit from selling the timber but they only get part of the ecosystem services. The benefits for the rest of the world are external to the society that makes decisions about the forest and are not taken into account. The result is called a 'market failure'.[1]

The market failure might be addressed by paying the forest owners for the carbon sequestered by their forests or, as in the REDD schemes,[2] for maintaining forests that would otherwise disappear. It is worth noticing that these schemes are based on a 'beneficiary pays' rather than the 'polluter pays' principle (Spangenberg and Settele, 2010).

This chapter is about how community forestry organizations are likely to do a better job of dealing with some externalities than conventional firms. Community forestry organizations can **internalize certain externalities**, resulting in a more efficient economy.

7.3   The Theory of Externalities

The theory of externalities is generally credited to A. C. Pigou (1928), who argued that externalities are almost everywhere. As a result, markets often fail and government interventions through regulation or taxation may be necessary. He applied the concept to, among other areas, fires cause by railroads and road congestion. The logic of externalities is central in the 1954 analysis of open-access fisheries by Scott Gordon (1954).

The theory of externalities can be, and has been, used to justify widespread government interventions in markets. There are noise bylaws, fines for dumping and polluting, laws about maintaining the appearance of one's property, zoning regulations, and hundreds of other examples. The best-known application of Pigou's ideas today is probably the growing use of carbon taxation to deal with global warming. The carbon tax is a 'Pigouvian corrective tax', designed to make markets work better.

Barnett and Yandle (2009) observe, however, that "all externality problems can be considered as property rights problems". The solution in this view is to reassign the property rights. If people in a gated community are dumping garbage over their walls, one solution is to give them the land around their community. Then they will care about the effect of their garbage on the people outside. Why will they care? Because they if they own the land they will want to maximize its value – perhaps to rent to outsiders. If they dump garbage they will get less rent money.

A common prescription in the economics of fisheries, described by Gordon (1954), is reassigning rights so that someone has a stake in maximizing the resource rent available from the fishery. The really means making some single entity the owner of the entire fishery. Forest tenure, seen as a set of property rights, is seriously misaligned with the full range of costs and benefits of forestry. The proposition underlying community forestry is that assigning property rights to the community will increase the economic efficiency of forest use.

Regulation, taxes, and reassigning property rights are all useful

The Theory of Externalities **85**

ways of dealing with some externalities and simply not workable in others. Sometimes the best policy is to do nothing because the cost of solving a problem is greater than the benefit it will produce. Zhang (2001) notes, for example, that "the costs associated with defining, protecting and transferring property rights in trees, land and products are much higher in forestry than in agriculture", suggesting that solving externality problems in forestry by privatization may be too costly.

Externalities are common in forestry and in communities. It is important to be able to identify externalities in both forestry operations and in community management, to be able to assess how serious they are, and to know something about the range of tools available for dealing with externalities.

7.3.1 *Prescription for Dealing with Externalities*

The basic rule in the theory of externalities is that the *sum* of the benefits and the *sum* of costs to all members of society must be counted, not just the benefits for a subgroup. Economic efficiency is achieved when the sum of the marginal benefits is set equal to the marginal costs.

$$\sum_i MB_i = \sum_i MC_i \qquad (7.1)$$

Equation 7.1 requires that costs and benefits across the entire population must be included when evaluating a project. If a project affects people in several ways – for example Roy cares about fishing, views, and where he parks his truck at the lake – we need to include all ways he is affected:

$$MB_{Roy} = \sum_{j\ effects} MB_{Roy}.$$

If the sum of benefits is greater than the sum of costs, a project is worth doing. If the benefits are less than the costs the project is not

86 *Externalities and Community Forestry*

worth doing. Notice that the sums in Equation 7.1 are not monetary costs and benefits. When an economist says the "sum of the costs" she is including every kind of cost. It may be useful to express non-monetary costs or benefits effect in dollars to make the comparison Equation 7.1 calls for, but the equation itself says nothing about money.

There is a slightly tricky detail about marginal I costs worth mentioning at this point. 'Marginal' means 'at the margin' or 'at the boundary'. A boundary is usually a thin line, and when we say marginal in economics we usually mean the result of an infinitesimally small change: a change that is the thickness of a line. In practice though, if we are considering, for example, clearcutting a section of land, the *total* revenue generated and the *total* environmental costs for the entire section should be included (as well as any other costs and benefits). These total effects *are* the marginal effects. Harvesting that particular section of land is the margin, or change, that we are considering. If we wanted, we could think about increasing the harvest area by just one square metre. For that decision, the costs and benefits from adding just that square metre would be the marginal benefits and costs to consider.

7.4   *Inter-community Externalities*

At the community level there may be externalities that affect non-members and externalities that affect members. Inter-community externalities include effects on shared watersheds, carbon sequestration, increases in wildlife or threats to species, and even the benefits provided to outsiders by local roads. Some of these have important economic effects. Carbon emissions or sequestration affect the entire globe, but they only matter economically when there is a possibility of being paid for sequestration or charged for emissions.

The UN's Clean Development Mechanism (CDM) and the REDD programme pay communities for providing external benefits. Under the CDM communities are funded for projects that reduce emissions. Under REDD they are paid for reforestations and retaining forests.

In both cases there is a superior governmental organization providing incentives that are supposed to offset market failures. These programmes present business opportunities at the community level. Qualifying can be difficult and costly.

When national or provincial governments deal with externalities they often employ regulation rather than economic incentives. Protecting habitat for endangered species often imposes costs on local governments and communities, if only by limiting timber harvest. It is justified on the grounds that the endangered species have value to the public in some way. Regulation is often cheaper than providing economic incentives. As with the UN programmes the interests of the wider public are represented by a higher-level government.

There are a few cases where non-governmental organizations (NGOs) have provided financial incentives to maintain forest. There are cases where environmental NGOs have actually purchased forests to protect them. The NGOs are operating as unelected representatives of the wider community. They rely on incentives in part because they don't have the legislative authority to use regulations.

Extra-community externalities can be important. They may become moral issues, as when a community undertakes to cut its CO_2 emissions to fight climate change. They become economic issues when there is a senior partner that can provide incentives or impose rules. When incentives or disincentives are used the senior partner is using Pigouvian taxes and subsidies to correct the price system.

7.5   Intra-community Externalities

Externalities matter because they come with opportunities for doing better. Within a community, externalities can be discussed and in some cases at least, ways may be found to make members of the community better off. Some cases are simple. If you mow your lawn early Sunday and I partied late Saturday, your noise may cause some serious harm. You might be just as happy mowing later or buying a push-mower. Problem solved, as long as the right information gets to the right person.

88 *Externalities and Community Forestry*

In forest communities many of the externalities of interest are related to forest production. Logging trucks are noisy and they damage public roads. If the logger is a private operator, eliminating the externalities may make him poorer. If the logger is owned by the community, community members can decide if the noise warrants limiting the hours that their trucks pass though town and if the damage to the road should be paid for out of logging revenues. There may be many solutions. Since the costs are paid for out of the same pocket the discussion is simpler. It isn't necessary to sign a contract or to bring in a new bylaw.

Conflict between cutting and recreational use can be resolved in a similar way. Community forestry has two advantages in this case. First, because the community is the property holder for the forestry operation, it may be possible to rearrange the rights of members to reduce conflict. Rearranging property rights is one the standard solutions for externality problems. Negotiating a solution may not be easy, but it will generally be easier than if rights were controlled outside of the community.

The second advantage for community forest organizations is that they have deliberative capacity – a community forest is, by the definition used in this analysis, a democratic form of local government with the responsibility for resolving conflicts arising from forest use.

For intra-community externalities, efficiency improvements come from both reassigning property rights and from reducing the costs of negotiating solutions. The second of these is closely related to the question of transaction costs taken up in Chapter 9.

Notes

[1]Calling this 'market failure', as many economists do, may suggest that markets are normally supposed to solve all allocation problems efficiently. Failing to deal with externalities could just as well be called 'governance failure' or 'erroneous reliance on markets'.

[2]Reducing Emissions from Deforestation and forest Degradation (REDD) is a mechanism that has been under negotiation by the United Nations Framework Convention on Climate Change (UNFCCC) since 2005, with the objective of mitigating the effects of climate change
through reducing net emissions of greenhouse gases through enhanced forest management in developing countries.

8
Public Goods and Public Forests

The theory of public goods demands a chapter in any book on the economics of community forestry. A public good is an asset or good that anyone can enjoy without reducing the amount available to others. Every community supplies a variety of public goods.

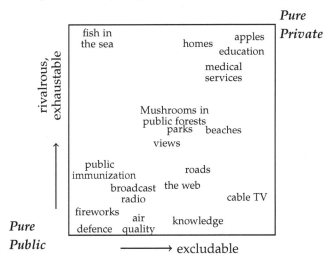

Figure 8.1: Public and private goods

Local roads, for example, can be used freely and, except at rush hour and at crowded intersections, riders, walkers and pedestrians rarely interfere with each other. Roads are used for street hockey and basketball by children, by retailers to make deliveries, and by municipal trucks to remove garbage.

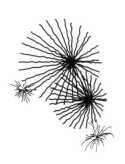

Figure 8.2: Public spectacles are public goods

Public goods, like fireworks displays for example, have two unusual economic properties. In the jargon of economics, a pure public good is "**non-excludable**": it is generally hard to exclude people from a public good. It is hard, for example, to prevent people from watching a public display of fireworks. A public good is also "**non-rival**", or "non-exhaustible": when one person uses a public good it is still available for others.

Goods with varying degrees of rivalrousness and excludability are illustrated in Figure 8.1. High enforcement cost can transform private goods into de facto public goods. For example, the front garden of your house, a private good, is enjoyed by your neighbours, making it effectively a public good.

A public good like a view is quite different from a pure private good like an apple or a 2x4s. When an apple is eaten no one else can eat it. A view is still there after I have looked at it. Efficiency requires that we count the benefits to everyone and set the total marginal benefit equal to the marginal cost of supply.

$$sum_i MB_i = MC \qquad (8.1)$$

The benefits to many people are balanced against the single expenditure needed to provide the public good.

Non-excludability and non-rivalrousness make it very difficult for markets to supply public goods efficiently. If you can't keep people from using what you produce it is hard to charge them for using it. Furthermore, if the product is non-rival, keeping people from enjoying it can't be efficient. But if you can't charge for a public good and you shouldn't charge for it, how will you pay for it? To some extent, roads, bridges, public radio and preventing climate change all present us with this dilemma.

Communities and forests both have public good features. This chapter explains some of the economic implications of this publicness for forest communities.

8.1   Some Examples

Before we consider public goods in community forestry it is worth looking at some of the puzzles and problems that public goods present.

8.1.1   Broadcast Media

Public broadcasters are a nearly perfect example of a public good. When a signal is broadcast, anyone with a receiver can pick it up. The broadcast is nearly perfectly non-excludable. It is also perfectly non-rivalrous. Even if millions are already listening to the morning news, one more news junky can always turn on her radio and hear exactly the same programme at exactly the same time with exactly the same amount of static.[1]

Radio and TV are not really perfectly non-excludable, however. In the United Kingdom a licence was required to possess a radio until 1971. In other words there was legal 'technology' that made it possible to charge for broadcasts. Households are still required to pay £145.50 for an annual licence to operate a colour TV. The licence fee solved a problem for the British Broadcasting service: if you can't exclude consumers from your product you may be able to charge them for a related product.

Commercial broadcasters found a different solution: instead of charging the consumers they charged advertisers for access to consumers. Advertisements reduced the value of the product, but it made radio, and later the web, profitable. This is not an ideal

94 *Public Goods and Public Forests*

solution from an economic point of view, but it was a financial success.

Sometimes there are purely technological solutions to the problem of publicness. Cable distribution made it easy for cable companies to charge customers for access. A variety of innovations made costly cable more attractive than free broadcast signals, and what was once a public good became a private good.

8.1.2 Roads

There is a similar problem with roads. Road are not pure public goods because it is possible to keep people off them. If you owned the only road between London and Oxford it would be fairly easy to charge drivers for using your road. As the road network and the number of trips expand it gets harder and more expensive to charge people for the use of roads. Exclusion is possible but costly.

A variety of devices are used to get around the cost of tolling a road. Most communities pay for local roads out of property taxes. The correlation between property value and trip generation is actually quite weak. Rural and suburban homes generate less tax revenue and more kilometres than similar urban homes. Vehicle taxes, used in many jurisdictions, also correlate poorly with use. Fuel taxes are fairly well correlated with distance travelled and vehicle weight so fuel taxes are often used to pay for roads. Unfortunately, increasing fuel efficiency and the introduction of electric vehicles weakens the correlation and makes the fuel tax a less effective way to finance roads. Improving technology is making it easier and cheaper to impose road tolls even in complex road networks.

Like parks, roads and highways are non-rival when few people are using them but become rival when heavily used. They get crowded. The crowding reduces the value of the good to all the users. Roads are therefore a *congestible* local public good With congestion, each user generates *negative externalities*: they cause delays and risks for other drivers. Congestion-sensitive road tolls can be used to correct for these externalities.

8.2 The Formal Theory of Public Goods

The central observation in public goods theory is that the value produced by a public good is the *sum* of the benefits to all members of the community. If the relevant benefit is the **sum** of individual benefits then the relevant marginal benefit is the sum of the individual marginal benefits. Since the standard economic efficiency condition is that marginal benefit should equal marginal cost, the Samuelson condition is simply

$$\sum_i MB_i = MC, \qquad (8.2)$$

where MB_i stands for the benefit for user i of the last unit provided.

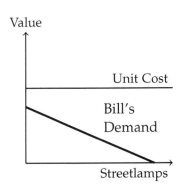

Figure 8.3: Bill's indiviudal demand for streetlamps

The efficiency rule expressed by Equation 8.2 can be illustrated using the familiar supply and demand diagram. The idea is simple. The height of a demand curve represents how much a person or collection of buyers value, for our example, an additional streetlight. Figures 8.3 and 8.4 illustrate the demand functions for two neighbours, Bill and Sue. The height of the heavy lines represent the marginal benefit each neighbour would get if another streetlight were provided.

MC stands for the marginal cost to society of providing the another light. It is shown as a the horizontal lines in Figures 8.3 and 8.4.

From Bill's point of view even one streetlight isn't worth its cost. Sue, however, would buy one streetlight. Her demand function in Figure 8.4 shows the benefit she would get from more street lighting.

It starts out higher than the cost of a streetlamp, so she comes out ahead if she buys a streetlamp. From Bill's demand function we know he would thank her, even though he wouldn't pay for street lighting on his own.

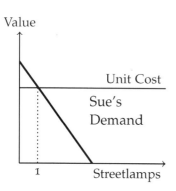

Figure 8.4: Sue's individual demands for streetlamps

The problem is that neither Bill nor Sue individually would provide the amount of streetlighting that Equation 8.2 prescribes.

The dashed line in Figure 8.5 represents the (vertical) *sum* of Sue and Bill's marginal benefits. The dashed line is produced by piling Sue's demand on top of Bill's. The dashed line corresponds to $\sum_i MB_i$. in Equation 8.2. Because they both benefit from the same streetlight their combined marginal benefit justifies buying twice as much as they would buy if they each purchased individually. They need to get together to provide streetlights efficiently.

Equation 8.2, illustrated in Figure 8.5, is a *prescription*: if we want an efficient allocation – if we want to maximize the benefits to society from the resources we have – this condition *must* be met.[2]

8.3 Preference Revelation and the Free-rider Problem

If Bill and Sue buy street lamps individually, Sue buys one and Bill doesn't. The decentralized solution is inefficient. Samuelson argued that "no decentralized pricing system can serve to determine optimally these levels of collective consumption".

If we could get Sue and Bill to tell us exactly how much benefit they receive from each new street lamps, the Samuelson condition could be used to calculate the optimal number. This would involve collecting private information and making a collective decision.

Preference Revelation and the Free-rider Problem

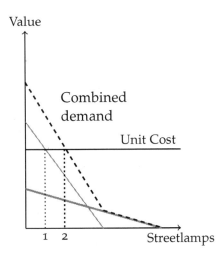

Figure 8.5: Summing the individual demand curves

At the optimal number of streetlights in Figure 8.5, Sue's demand is above Bill's. She values the last street light more than Bill does. Charging both the same price would leave Bill complaining that he didn't think the last light was worth the price. We could ask Bill and Sue separately how much they are willing to pay. Unfortunately, both know that the reason we are asking is so that we can charge each person an appropriate share of the cost. In this situation each has an incentive to understate the benefit they expect to receive. Asking directly gives each an opportunity to do so.

The problem of getting honest information when respondents have an incentive to misrepresent is known as the *preference revelation problem*. It is a major problem for any group, and it arises whenever there are public goods to be paid for. If community decision-makers do not have "full knowledge of individual preferences." it's likely that public goods will be under- or over-supplied.

Individuals who misrepresent the benefits they receive in order to avoid paying their share for a public good are said to be *free-riders* and finding ways to avoid losses due to free-riding is the *free-rider*

98 *Public Goods and Public Forests*

problem. The term seems to come from an illustration used in economics classes.[3] To save the cost of having a conductor collecting fares on a bus, a public transit system asked each riders to voluntarily contribute an amount equal to the value of the ride for them. Not surprisingly some riders contributed nothing. They misrepresented their preferences, in effect saying the ride had no value for them. The result, according to the story, is that the bus company went bankrupt and no one enjoyed the public good.

Public goods are closely related to Externalities.[4] With a public good the producer can't prevent others from enjoying the good. With an externality, others can't help consuming the good. With a public good the producer can't get paid. A producer who generates a positive externality also can't get paid. If I put flowers in my front garden my neighbours can enjoy them, but I still have to pay the entire cost. Unless I really love my neighbours I am likely to plant fewer flowers than an inclusive economic calculation calls for. With a negative externality the producer does not automatically pay for the damage done to others.

8.4 Public Goods and Community Forestry

There are two questions about public goods in the economics of community forestry. First, how should a community forest be managed when there are public goods? Second, could community forestry deal with public goods problems any more effectively than, for example, the conventional approach to managing public forests, public ownership with leases to forest companies?

We can limit the discussion to local public goods. Local forests certainly sequester carbon and they have an 'option value'[5] for non-residents, but these effects are more easily treated as externalities. They also have to be negotiated with governments or outside organizations.

Virtually every self-governing community provides public and quasi-public goods as well as excludable goods such as sports fields, swimming pools, hospitals, and schools. Community forestry does not introduce new issues until the forests are involved.

Forest roads, for example may provide access to lakes, hunting, camping and fishing opportunities, as well as scenery, shelter for cottages and tourism operations, usually without reducing the value of the harvest and without significantly increasing the costs of forest management. These uses draw on aspects of the forest with varying degrees of publicness. To achieve efficient use of the forest, all of these benefits must be taken into account.

Private operators cannot easily 'monetize' these benefits under current forest tenures because they cannot collect a fee equal to the marginal benefit they are generating for others. As a result, they provide less of the unvalued public benefits than society would like. This is one way markets are often inefficient. Privatizing forest land is sometimes proposed as a solution, but it would be necessary to privatize the public benefits as well to get managers to fully consider them, and that seems to be a step in the wrong direction. Governments can regulate, to try to force private managers to supply the correct amount of public goods – for example to open roads for recreational use.

With respect to the provision of local public goods, community forestry comes closest to being a situation where decisions are made by the people most affected.[6] Good decisions about local public goods require good information about what local people want. Local institutions are best placed to generate that information, and most likely to act on it.

There are risks in assigning more decision-making power to the local level. Communities might be exchanging market failure for political failure. There may be cases where local governments respond less effectively than senior government or more slowly than private firms. More often, community forestry organizations will be able to adapt their operations and rules to expand public access for members with as little risk to efficiency as possible.

Notes

[1] But notice even this nearly perfect example depends on having a transmitter nearby. The radio is a **local** public good. It isn't really available to everyone everywhere.

[2] Samuelson (1954) expressed the result in terms of marginal rates of transformation.

[3] In another version the first rider had to pay the full cost of the bus and all subsequent passengers rode for free. (Intellectual Property and Open Source: A Practical Guide to Protecting Code, by Van Lindberg)

[4] Liability law helps deal with some negative externalities. If it can be proved to the satisfaction of the court that harm has been done, the producer may be forced to pay the cost of the harm. Knowing that he will have to pay often discourages a producer from generating harm.

[5] Option value refers to the value that is placed on private willingness to pay for maintaining or preserving a public asset or service even if there is little or no likelihood of the individual actually ever using it.

[6] The principle that social problems should be dealt with at the most immediate (or local) level consistent with their solution is known as Subsidiarity.

Part III

COMMUNITY

9
Transaction Cost Theory and Community Forestry

As interest in community forestry grows there has been a sharp rise in the number of studies applying the theory of the firm to this unfamiliar enterprise form. A recent theme in this literature is the role of transaction costs. With few exceptions (e.g., Wang and van Kooten, 1999), studies consider community forestry enterprises in developing countries, such as China (Zhang, 2001), Nepal (Adhikar and Lovett, 2006, Rai, Bigsby and MacDonald), Tanzania (Meshack et al., 2006), Uganda (Wasswa-Matovu, 2010), or Mexico (Vega and Keenan, 2014).

Transaction costs are found to have various effects. Zhang (2001), for example, examines the role of community forestry in reducing transaction costs in China. Wasswa-Matovu (2010) examines how transaction costs are a barrier to community forestry in Uganda. Vega and Keenan (2014) examine how transaction costs influence vertical integration and governance in Mexican community forest enterprises.[1] Others emphasize high transactions costs making access to capital or dealing with regulations difficult for smaller community forestry organizations. In this chapter we'll look at transaction cost theory (TCT) and what it can tell us about community forestry.

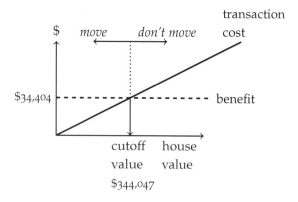

Figure 9.1: Transaction costs may exceed the value of a transaction

9.1 The History of Transaction Costs Theory

In 1931 John R. Commons (1931) pointed out that "the smallest unit of the institutional economists is a unit of activity – a transaction, with its participants". He described an emphasis on transactions as marking "the transition from the classical and hedonic schools to the institutional schools of economic thinking". The approach of the institutionalist school is to look at how organizations affect economic behaviour. The focus is shifted from market behaviour and prices to legal structures, contracts, information and governance. Commons suggested that analysis should focus on "the alienation and acquisition, between individuals, of the rights of property and liberty created by society, which must therefore be negotiated between the parties concerned before labor can produce, or consumers can consume, or commodities be physically exchanged".

The term 'transaction costs' became prominent in the literature on the Coase 'theorem' (Coase, 1937) beginning in the 1960s. In his 1937 paper and later Coase never went beyond providing examples of transaction costs, did not use the term 'transaction costs' and gave a very brief, even cryptic definition. The 'theorem', never explicitly stated by Coase, proposed that "In the absence of transaction costs, the allocation of resources is independent of the distribution of property rights" (Allen, 2000). Cheung (1969) generalized this argument to the context of contracts and contract choice. The argument depends on the obviously false assumption that there are no transaction costs: clearly if transaction costs are too high some beneficial exchanges may not happen. The eventual result of Coase's controversial claim was the launch of a concerted study of transaction costs in the 1970s (see Williamson (2010)).

Emphasizing the need to negotiate before producing, and on rights created by society, focussed attention on the kind of institutions (firms, markets, franchises, etc.) that minimize the transaction costs of producing and distributing goods or services. It gave rise to a school of institutional economics which argues that societies can only survive if they create institutions that reduce transaction costs (North and Thomas, 1973). Since community forestry is based on shifting tenure rights to local communities, a move to community forestry is likely to affect transaction costs. Meshack et al. (2006) point out "Transaction costs are critical factors in the success or failure of Community Based Forest Management and need to be incorporated into policies and legislation related to community-based natural resource management".

9.2   The Idea of Transaction Costs

The basic concept of a transaction cost is simple. Imagine that you want to move to a house with the same market value as the house you own, but nearer your work. The new location would save you 40 minutes a day for 20 years – a value of perhaps $12 a day or $2,400 a year. If you could be bothered to do the calculation you might conclude that the saving has a total present value of $31,404.77, discounting at 5%.

In principle this is a simple transaction. You are exchanging one house for another. In practice you will pay a real estate agent, a lawyer, and a company to move your possessions out of the house. You will spend many hours making sure the house will show well,

106 *Transaction Cost Theory and Community Forestry*

hours arranging to transfer your mortgage and hours preparing the new house. You even spend time changing your address at the post office. These are all real costs.

Say the monetary and non-monetary costs of exchanging houses add up to 10% of the value of your house. If your house is worth more than $314,047.70, these transaction costs will be greater than the saving from moving. Figure 9.1 shows transaction costs rising as the value of the house rises until they exceed the benefits of a move.

The example shows that high transactions costs might make a productive transaction uneconomic. Surprisingly, a great deal of economic analysis implicitly assumes zero transaction costs.[2] In Chapter 6, for example, Pareto efficiency was defined as a situation where no reallocation can make anyone better off without making someone else worse off. Any reallocation involves a transaction, but the definition doesn't say "no reallocation can make anyone better off *after paying any transactions costs* without making someone else worse off".

9.3 Transaction Cost Theory

Transaction Cost Theory (TCT) more generally is about the economics of organization. Oliver Williamson, a pioneer of formal modelling in the field, argues that governance is the overarching concept and transaction cost economics is the "means by which to breathe operational content into governance and organization" (Williamson, 2010). In practice, transaction cost theory usually focusses on the way certain forms of organization reduce transaction costs. A major insight of TCT is that the need to reduce transaction costs may drive vertical integration.

In the forest industry, for example, control of the land base, harvest planning, harvesting, transportation, mills, marketing and finance all may come under a single management. Figure 9.2 provides a very simple view of transaction costs in a forest product supply chain. Functions are performed by small firms that are essentially command economies. Their internal transaction costs are low.

Transaction Cost Theory 107

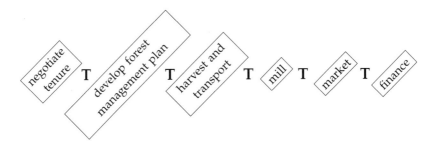

Figure 9.2: Hypothetical management units and transactions

Transaction costs, T, *between* firms are likely to be significant, and the more stages there are, the larger the potential savings from vertical integration.

In Figure 9.3 all the external negotiated transactions in the supply chain have been replaced by command relationships internal to the firm. The cost saving of roughly $5(T - t)$ provides a sense of how transaction costs might drive vertical integration. $T - t$ can represent person-hours, person-days or even person-years.

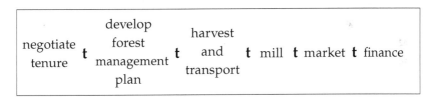

Figure 9.3: Transaction costs decline with vertical integration

Figure 9.4 suggests a more complex structure resulting from horizontal mergers. Vertical integration reduces the transaction costs. Mergers allow firms to provide management services, deal with government for tenure rights, plan and make decisions about financing and planning centrally. Functions on the right are shared by all units. Costs are reduced by combining the management functions for several production units, resulting in economies of scale.

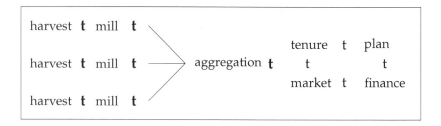

Figure 9.4: Transactions costs with mergers

9.4 Transaction Costs in Practice

Transaction costs do not seem to be a barrier to community ownership of forests. In fact the opposite is true. Zhang (2001) argues that the high share of public forests in the world can be explained best in terms of transaction costs. Public ownership, and by extension, community forestry tenure, which is functionally just local public ownership, results in less cost required in defining and transferring the property rights.

The transaction costs in dealing wth harvesters are not a barrier to community forestry. The actual harvesting in most North American forests is often done by small contractors, many of whom own or lease equipment. This suggests that the efficient boundary between firm and the market for forestry companies might lie at the level of the mill. Mystic Management, for example, is a First Nations-owned forestry operation in Saskatchewan that controlled 16% of the annual allowable cut for the province in 2006.[3] It owns one mill and supplies another. Mystic actively works to develop a system of small contractors from local First Nations communities. All that is required is for community forestry organizations to have the ability to subcontract work, a capacity every municipal government already has.[4]

There is a great deal of other evidence that commercial mills don't need to control harvesting nor land. US mills typically buy logs on an open market. In Europe more than 80% of private forest in Europe is held by individuals or families. In Finland, Austria, France, Iceland, Norway, Slovenia and the UK, the majority of the harvested forest is held privately, and in Finland 56% of the total forests is held by families (Hirsch, Korotkov, and Wilnhammer, 2007). Companies that own forest lands in the US are selling their forest holdings to corporations that hold the forests as financial assets (Temperate Forest Foundation, 2006; Clutter et al. (2005)).[5] It does not appear that transaction cost arguments can be used to support corporate forest tenure.

There seems to be some agreement that operating with a small forest does not induce excessive transaction costs when it come to marketing wood as long as local log markets are reasonably competitive. Mills throughout the US rely on small producers. In some areas where there are few mills or mills are widely spaced mill operators may exploit their market power either to underpay or to tie producers to themselves (see Benner, Lertzman, and Pinkerton (2014)).

External transaction costs in forestry are not limited to dealing with markets, however. In many cases complex regulatory frameworks impose large transactions costs on local forestry producers (Scherr, White, and Kaimowitz., 2004), in part because commercial forestry production tends to be more regulated than other economic sectors due to concerns for forest conservation (Larson et al., 2008). There are apparent scale economies in negotiating tenure and dealing with regulators. Under the legislation in Ontario, for example, firms must present a forest management plan every five years.

Since there are substantial fixed costs involved in dealing with the Ministry, these transaction costs introduce an economy of scale that favours larger firms. Furthermore, it is a cost that depends on reporting requirements, which are determined by regulators. This 'economy' has nothing to do with production efficiency, and might be considered a market distortion. If regulators made the transaction costs of planning and permitting proportional to harvest area they would remove an artificial bias in favour of large holders. Although community forests are currently much smaller than most industrial tenures, they are much larger than most family tenures in Europe and larger than most woodlots in the North America. If compliance, regulation and transaction costs for European family-held forests are manageable, it seems likely that the same costs can be brought in line for community forests.

There are said to be significant economies in obtaining finance as well, another example of a transaction cost that encourages the creation of large organizations. Here too a market imperfection is responsible for a bias against community forestry.

9.5 Transaction Costs in Community Forestry

The descriptions so far seem to leave little room for a transaction cost argument in favour of community forestry. Vertical integration may be difficult for community forestry organizations, giving commercial operations a significant advantage. Vega and Keenan (2014) suggest that they may even be subject to higher transaction costs than a private operator: "Communities that want to benefit from commercial forestry face considerable transaction costs in their relationships with external service providers and buyers. Opportunistic behaviour from buyers and contractors to secure additional rents can occur at all levels of vertical integration". Several authors have argued that transaction costs are prohibitively high for community forest organization in developing countries. "Generally, it can be concluded that forestry regulations tend to operate against the interest of communities and smallholders because they impose both legal barriers and transactions costs to them", according to Cornejo et al. (n.d.). Skutsch (2004) observes that "community forest management projects are small scale, and the transaction costs associated with justifying them as climate projects are likely to be high".[6]

Examining the arguments made for community forestry and for aboriginal control of forests, however, it is clear that supply chain efficiency is not the focus of most advocates. Much more common are arguments based on diversification of the local economy, local employment, and employment stability. These arguments appear to revolve around more effective and more flexible use of the local resources. They rely on economies of scope not available to most commercial firms. These include the possibility of carbon sequestration projects (Skutsch, 2004), use of non-commercial timber, craft and speciality wood products and Non-Timber Forest Products (NTFPs) such as mushrooms, wild rice, herbs, fruits, nuts roots, fungi, maple syrup, birch syrup, blueberries, ferns, pharmaceuticals.[7] Tourism and recreational uses of forest land are also local products that may provide income locally but are not currently a concern of industrial tenure holders. These activities are typically small-scale and seasonal. They do require reliable forest access, scheduling and land-use planning, which may threaten a company that produces volume commodities.

These non-standard and non-timber forest products have not been of interest to forestry firms, perhaps because they might interfere with industrialized harvests and perhaps because it is difficult to achieve economies of scale and they require intensive use of local information. In addition, according to Whiteman (2003), "Although many surveys may indicate that forests can produce outputs with high non-financial values, and although economic theory shows that these values should be reflected in the utilization of the forest resource, the cost of trying to create markets for these outputs will have a major effect on whether such attempts will work or not". They are frequently mentioned among potential economic gains for proposed and existing community forests.

The ability to exploit economies of scope in community forestry may depend on reduced transaction costs. The distinction, discussed above, between internal and external transaction costs, focusses on the boundary between the firm and the market. Another useful distinction emphasizes specific activities that support exchange. There are three broad groups of functional costs that may be reduced for community forestry organizations:

- Search and information costs
- Bargaining costs

112 *Transaction Cost Theory and Community Forestry*

- Policing and enforcement costs

A community forest may have significant advantages with respect to all three costs.

9.5.1 *Advantages in Search and Information Gathering*

Resident members of a community forest are likely to have a great deal more local information than non-resident or temporarily assigned managers. Furthermore they are likely to exchange information more freely with each other than would occur if they were in a hierarchical organization (see Chapter 10 to see how this process can drive innovation). They also have a stake in information exchange that leads to local employment or quality of life improvements. As a consequence they may be more likely to make an effort to match an opportunity with a member of the community and more likely to promote an initiative even if it does not contribute to the bottom line of thee main community enterprise.

These informational activities are relatively cheap for small communities. For hierarchically organized forestry firms attempting to exploit small local economic opportunities, internal transaction costs for innovation are relatively large. In fact, the firm's effort to minimize costs by reducing staff and increasing time-on-task is likely reduce the likelihood that small and local projects will be identified and undertaken.

Community forestry could therefore enjoy lower transaction costs with respect to search and information than a commercial operation. These advantages might partially offset the advantages available to commercial operation through vertical integration and mergers. Chapter 10 formalizes these arguments to demonstrate that community-based forestry has the potential to innovate in part because of the high density of within-community linkages.

9.5.2 *Advantages in Bargaining and Contracting*

The second category of transaction costs – the costs of bargaining – are also likely to be lower for community forestry for several reasons.

First, research on bargaining games suggests that goodwill and altruism contribute to efficient and equitable outcomes. Goodwill and altruism are features of non-market transactions and they can both reduce the time required to reach agreement and reduce the need for detailed formal agreements.

Second, frequent interaction and knowledge about ones bargaining partner can also reduce bargaining costs. Repeated interaction can generate conventions, often tacit, that simplify negotiation. Furthermore, when know each other's 'bottom lines', or 'threat points', to use the language of Nash bargaining theory, it is easier to identify acceptable solutions.

Third, members of a community may be willing to spend more time and care getting to an agreement simply because discussion, including gossip is a rewarding social activity. A great deal of the thinking in community organizations is actually unpaid recreational activity, which may give community forests a cost advantage over normal firms.

Finallly, because there are many links within the community, there are likely to be more possible trades to bring to the table, including non-monetary considerations.

9.5.3   Advantages with Respect to Trust and Compliance

Ostrom and others have argued that in common property situations, including forestry, one requirement for success is that resources be devoted to monitoring whether people comply and to enforcing the decisions of the community if they don't comply. Policing and enforcement reduces the chance that people will renege on agreements or simply steal form the common pool. In small communities social norms may serve to enforce a reasonable standard of behaviour. Members of a community forest organization all have a stake in the organization, and many are likely to participate voluntarily in monitoring and enforcement. With sufficient community engagement monitoring costs will be lower for a community forest organization than for a private owner.

9.6 Conclusion

These advantages with respect to transaction cost are not automatic. Community forestry organizations will have to consciously work to minimize transaction costs. They will have to devote resources to keeping communications flowing, maintaining trust, and making sure that norms of behaviour are understood. Interestingly, while these activities are genuine costs, they also appear as increased human and social capital – as capacity building that is likely to generate unexpected benefits.

Comparing transaction costs for organizational systems operating under different regulatory regimes is clearly a risky project, especially when one of the systems is still being invented. As Coase (1960) pointed out, in general "the interrelationships which govern the mix of market and hierarchy are extremely complex and in our present state of ignorance it will not be easy to discover what these factors are".[8]

Conventional forestry firms operate within a legal and regulatory structure that has its roots in colonial times. Firms have participated in shaping the rules and are integrated with the regulatory bureaucracies in several ways. There is currently no similarly developed system of rules and conventions for community forestry.[9] Widespread and well-established community forestry would develop techniques to exploit their informational advantages. There is no way of knowing at this stage of community forestry development whether the transaction cost advantages of community forestry outweigh the different transaction cost advantages of industrial forestry.

The tenure regime within which community forestry operates will have an impact on the structure and size of transaction costs. It will be essential, if community forestry is to succeed, to establish rules that minimize transaction costs.

Notes

[1]"Obtaining legally valid documents and permits, usufruct rights in the form of forest concessions or extractive reserves, as well as constituting formal smallholder organizations involved lengthy processes with high transaction costs, even more as government norms and regulations often were relatively difficult to comply with. Where some kind of certification was pursued, this also proved to be an equally cumbersome and expensive undertaking". Jong et al. (2010)

[2]" ... the distribution of transaction costs across various sub-groups of resource users is generally not incorporated into an economic analysis of participatory forest management, leading to failure of communal efforts". Wasswa-Matovu (2010)

[3]Second Report on First Nations Forest Tenures in Canada. (NAFA, 2007).

[4]"Small contractors" may own or lease several million dollars worth of harvesting or road-building equipment. Miscellaneous 2015 examples make the point. A 2004 John Deere 748GIII Dual Arch Grapple Skidder with 26,605 hours showing on the metre sells for $65,000 Canadian. A 2014 Peterbilt 289 log truck with a Rotobec Loader might go for $190,000. A 2008 used TimberPro feller bunches was selling for $290,000. A 2014 CAT 501HD Harvester was listed at $399,000.

[5]The fact is that forest management is often not profitable. In addition, because of the long-term nature of forest management, investment in forestry can be risky and tends to be less attractive to investors than other, shorter-term enterprises. Editorial, *Unasylva* 212, Vol. 54, 2003

[6]Transaction costs for idealized community forest organizations are compared to the transaction costs for idealized conventional forestry firms in Chapter 10.

[7]Some examples if NTFPs pursued by First Nation forest communities are described in "Innovative Aboriginal Tenures: Non-timber forestry products, forest activities as a result of political races and conservation activities". National Aboriginal Forestry Association, 2012

[8]Coase seems to have considered firms and markets as the only available alternatives.

[9]There is a legislative framework in British Columbia, for example, but the terms of tenure and the regulatory mechanisms are variations on those developed for industrial forestry. They are likely to evolve significantly as the community forestry sector develops.

10
The Creative Potential of Community Forestry: The Small World Phenomenon

Business and government are obsessed with innovation. Innovation is held up as the key to profits and the path to growth. If community forestry is to compete politically with the industry incumbents it will have to promise more than social justice and a slightly better environmental stewardship. It will have to demonstrate a capacity to innovate that at least compares to the current system.

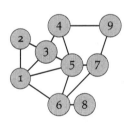

Figure 10.1: A network graph

Among the claims made for community forestry are that it can promote local economic development, make local economies more resilient and diverse, use forest resources more effectively, and advance the development of non-timber forest products. These are essentially claims that community forestry organizations would innovate in ways that conventional firms do not.

Network theory has been developed to think about the pattern of links in organizations. An extensive literature (e.g., Christopherson,

118 *The Creative Potential of Community Forestry*

Kitson, and Michie (2008), Inkpen and Tsang (2005), Burt (1992), Song, Chen, and Zhang (2014), Ritala, Gnyawali, and Järvi (2014)) has emerged on regional, intra-firm and inter-firm innovation networks. Innovation at the community level has been neglected, possibly.

The agent-based network model in this chapter[1] provides a way to assess a number of the economic claims made for community forestry relative to conventional industrial forestry. Comparing a stylized community forest networks to a stylized forestry company networks, we find that community forestry, at least in theory, can mobilize the innovation potential of a community *more* effectively than the dominant forest tenure system.

There is a tendency to think of community forestry organizations in much the way we think about standard firms. Seen as a network, community forestry differs in at least three important ways from the more familiar corporate management model for forests.

- The pattern of links among the members of the community differs from the pattern of links among employees in conventional corporate forestry.
- Incentives for decision-makers differ.
- Participation in decision-making differs.

These differences are the basis of an innovation advantage for community forestry.

10.1   What is Innovation?

There are many kinds of innovation. Discovering new uses and new markets for an available set of resources is very different from finding new and cheaper ways of producing the same product.[2] The first – call it *product innovation* – creates jobs. The second – call it *process innovation*, generally involves reducing employment in forestry. The distinction, crude as it is, is important for policy makers and for forest-based communities.

The dominant form of tenure in Canada's forestry system encourages process innovation. Labour is replaced with capital, reducing labour demand and threatening forest communities. Community

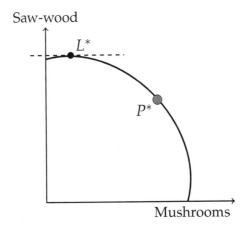

Figure 10.2: A multi-product, multi-interest forest

forestry, as this chapter will show, may be much more efficient at generating product innovation and would therefore strengthen forest communities.

For example, a region might support both logging and marketing forest mushrooms.[3] A logging company would value only sawlogs and would produce at L^*. However, if the local community held the right to manage the forest and to appropriate the gains, it might discover the possibility of marketing mushrooms and choose to produce at P^*, with a lower saw-log output but a higher total value. In Figure 10.2, any positive price for mushrooms would tilt the dashed line down toward the right and shift the efficient output combination to the right along the production possibilities curve. In other words, any positive price would make mushroom production worthwhile. Process innovation and capital investment over time would naturally reduce the labour required to produce L^*, making alternative income more important for the community.

Another innovation available to a community forestry organization might be to employ waste wood for district heating. Community members would naturally consider domestic heating as legitimate concern, while a forestry company would see district heating as a new business that is outside of its core competencies and difficult to manage.

A third value-adding innovation available to a community forestry organization could be producing fine grained woods for instrument-making. A small-scale enterprise such as this would be of little interest to a firm producing commodity sawn timber and paying industrial wages. It is likely to require specialized skills and marketing efforts that a forest products firm would lack. It could be of interest to a community because they offer a certain amount of diversification and off-season employment. It might be attractive to individual members of the community with an interest in self-employment.

10.2 Some Network Theory

Formally, a network is a mathematical object consisting of nodes and links between nodes, called edges. The nodes can represent people and the edges can represent the relationships between people.

Social networks are really the skeleton of a community. They are credited with a remarkable range of effects, including:

1. Networks create social capital for individuals (Burt (1997), Burt (1992), and Bourdieu (1986)) and communities (Putnam (2000) and Portes and Sensenbrenner (1993)).
2. Network forms of organization are an alternative to markets and hierarchies (Powell (1990)).
3. Networking appears to be one means of overcoming issues of access related to scale, as well as the transfer of knowledge and other factors relevant to environmental and economic sustainability (Glasmeier and Farrigan (2005)).
4. Networks are the defining feature of "innovative regions" such as Silicon Valley (Saxenian (1994), Owen-Smith and Powell (2004), Fleming, King, and Juda (2007)).
5. Networks are the locus of innovation in high-technology industries (Powell, Koput, and Smith-Doerr (1996), Stuart, Hoang, and Hybels (1999), Ahuja (2000), Owen-Smith, Riccaboni, et al. (2002)).
6. Networks create trust and increase forebearance (Piore and Sabel (1984) and Uzzi (1997)).

7. Networks shape the diffusion of technologies (Rodgers (1962); Coleman et al (1966)).

(Adapted from Jason Owen-Smith, Network Theory: The Basics. a presentation for the OECD)

Not all the nodes in a network have to be connected, just as in a community not everyone talks to each other person in the community. Nodes and edges can vary. Some notes might represent people who have more information than others. Some edges might represent regular and reliable communication while other represent very occasional communication.

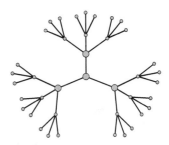

Figure 10.3: A hierarchical network

The most significant ways that a community forest network will differ from the network of a conventional corporate forestry are

- **Membership:** In a community forest organization a large fraction of the community is likely to be involved in decision-making. Membership would include non-employees, retired persons and a variety of public servants. In the network of a firm only a subset of the community is strongly connected to the firm. For a firm operating in several communities, similar subsets of each community will be linked through management across communities. The diversity of members is likely to be lower: in forestry communities, the employees are predominantly working-aged males.
- **The pattern of links:** Most conventional firms are hierarchically organized and can be modelled as a simple **balanced tree** as in Figure 10.3. Decision-making tends to be centralized and major decisions may occur outside of the community. Worker engagement, especially in decision-making, is usually limited. In a community forestry organization links are more random, often denser, and decision-making occurs within the community.
- **Incentives:** Members of a community may value local products that do not provide profit for a forestry company. The community

may value the stability and the level of of employment. Increasing employment is not a goal for firms. This is one of the fundamental features of community forestry described in Chapter 4 that gave rise to efficiency gains.

We can model a community forest as a **small-world network**, a graph in which most nodes are not neighbours of one another, but most nodes can be reached from every other by a small number of steps.

The key features of a small world network are

1. Links among network nodes are globally sparse: most people are not directly connected
2. There is high local clustering of links: most people are connected in groups with many connections among the members. Figure 10.4 shows a regular lattice that satisfies conditions 1 and 2.
3. Although the network may contain a large number of nodes, any pair of nodes in the network is typically linked by a short path: everyone knows someone who knows someone who knows you. The length of the shortest path between any two people is much shorter than the average path length.

Figure 10.4: A simple lattice

In other words, in a small world there are shortcuts. Figure 10.4 shows a simple lattice in which each node is connected to four neighbours. It is constructed by starting with a circle of n nodes. Then each node in the ring is connected with its k nearest neighbours (k-1 neighbours if k is odd). The number k is the *degree* of the graph. In a large network of this sort, average distances can be large even though individual nodes are tightly connected.

Watts and Strogatz (1998) showed that rewiring of a small percentage of the edges in a lattice results in a precipitous decrease in the path length, but only trivial reductions in the clustering. They also demonstrated that this 'small world' structure supports efficient information transfer. Figure 10.5 shows a lattice with shortcuts added and a random graph in which immediate neighbours are not necessarily connected but average distances are small.

 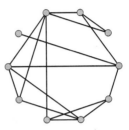

Figure 10.5: A small world graph and a random graph

Watts-Strogatz graphs are created from a simple lattice by randomly *replacing* some edges with links to randomly chosen nodes. This random rewiring[4] keeps the number of links constant, simplifying comparisons (the degree, k, is uniform). For example edge u-v is detached from v and attached to a randomly chosen node w. The Watts-Strogatz graph was the first to reliably generate clustering close to that of a lattice and path lengths similar to those of random networks.

Real-world networks have been found to have heavy-tailed degree distributions, which means that there are usually a few agents with a with very high number of connections. These highly connected individuals, or 'linkers', can make the network even more efficient.

10.3 A Model

Innovation in a community with local knowledge can be seen as a treasure hunt. The hidden treasures are units of local knowledge, skills, leadership, and even links to outside sources, that are capable of being combined into projects. The 'letters' $\{a, b, c, ..\}$ standing for specific units of knowledge are scattered randomly across a

124 *The Creative Potential of Community Forestry*

network with 341 nodes. A single node can receive more than one letter (corresponding in a rough way to the possibility that some agent might know more than one useful fact at the beginning of the process).

A potential innovation is 'discovered' when any agent 'collects' all of the 'letters' needed for a particular project. For example, the letters $\{c, d, e\}$ might represent one opportunity and $\{l, m, n, o, p\}$ might represent another. The longer the sequence the more difficult it will be to assemble a complete sequence.

One of the strings in a required sequence might represent finding an entrepreneur capable of making the project work. In that case we can assume, without much loss of generality, that any opportunity is acted on as soon as it is completely identified.

Innovations are projects that create local jobs. An innovation may generate 2, 4, 8, 16 or 32 jobs. Innovations that generate more jobs are harder to find: they usually require collecting of more letters. Smaller innovations are more common and may be easy or difficult to find. A joint distribution of value (jobs) and difficulty (number of letters) is shown in Table 10.1.

Table 10.1: Joint distribution of jobs and string lengths

	Number of Letters				
Jobs	2	3	4	5	6
32					1
16				1	1
8			1	1	1
4		1	1	1	1
2	1	1	1	1	1

The table describes a community with $\sum_1^5 i = 15$ potential innovations. The total number of elements to be found is $(1 \times 2) + (2 \times 3) + (3 \times 4) + (4 \times 5) + (5 \times 6) = 70$. The number of potential jobs that result from the innovation available is $32 + 2 \times 16 + 3 \times 8 + 4 \times 4 +$

$2 \times 2 = 114$. These numbers are obviously arbitrary, but the pattern is plausible.

10.3.1 Search

Search is a process of visiting neighbours and sharing information. In each time period each agent visits each adjacent node with probability p_v. This can be seen as the probability of having a meaningful discussion with each neighbour or friend in a given period about potential projects and the resources needed for them. If people are strongly motivated to seek information that would create jobs, the probability of visits, p_v, will be higher. While visiting each neighbour, the probability of encountering the neighbour's neighbour is also p_v. This is consistent with empirical evidence that indicates attrition in social networks is roughly constant (Dodd, Muhamad, and Watts (2003)). If a neigbour is three links away, the probability that an agent visits that link in any period is p_v^3.

Agents have good memories in this model. Each agent remembers all the resources they have identified in all previous rounds. Furthermore each agent learns everything known by the agents they visit. After each round agents examine the collection of strings that they have accumulated and identify any complete projects. When an agent has collected all the pieces for an innovation, the innovation is then recorded as having been made in that interval. Each innovation can be made only one time. The process is repeated until all the innovations have been made. Since the network is connected and finite, every resource will eventually be found, and eventually every innovation will be achieved. If opportunities are scarce individual innovations will on average take a long time. If the network is a small world we expect a relatively rapid rate of innovation. The rate of innovation will depend on the probability of rewiring, p_w, and the probability, p_v, of visiting a neighbour.

This structure gives us a natural 'efficiency' measure: the fraction of potential innovations discovered. In round one there are 15 undiscovered innovations that can create 114 jobs. That number will fall to zero over time. The upper line in Figure 10.6 shows the growth of employment over 800 periods for one simulation. The lower line is the number of opportunities identified, or, since opportunities are always immediately exploited, the number of new enterprises established.

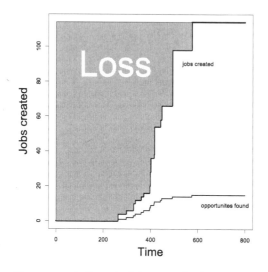

Figure 10.6: Sample history of job creation

The sum over time of still-undiscovered innovations,

$$\text{Loss} = \sum_{time}\sum_{jobs} (jobs\ not\ yet\ found\ at\ t), \qquad (10.1)$$

can be used as a performance measure. The lower this value is the more quickly the network finds all the possible jobs. In Figure 10.6 it corresponds to the shaded area above the upper line and below a horizontal line at 114 jobs. The other measure we will use is the time taken to discover all opportunities. In Figure 10.6 that is about 650 periods.

10.4 Comparing Time to Complete the Treasure Hunt in Small Worlds and Hierarchies

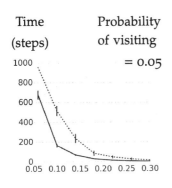

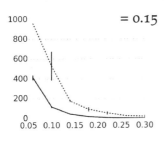

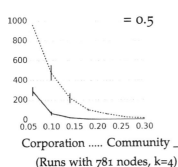

Corporation ..... Community ___
(Runs with 781 nodes, k=4)

Figure 10.7: Time steps to find all innovations

Figure 10.7 shows the average number of rounds needed to find all the jobs as a function of the probability of visiting for randomly generated networks. Trees and small worlds have the same number of nodes, and nodes have the same number of links. The three figures represent different probabilities of rewiring.

The average number of periods number required find all the opportunities is on the vertical axis. It falls steadily in all models as the probability of rewiring (and hence the average number of shortcuts) increases. The plots are averages for randomly generated trees and small worlds with the same number of nodes having the same number of links. The three figures represent different probabilities of rewiring.

The lower line in each panel of Figure 10.7 is the small world result. The upper, dotted line is the result for a comparable hierarchy. The small world is much faster at finding all the opportunities than the tree that represents the corporate hierarchical form of organization.

128 *The Creative Potential of Community Forestry*

10.4.1 Comparing Losses in Small Worlds and Hierarchies

The results are the same when we look at loss measures. Figure 10.8 plots the average loss (given by the Loss function in Equation 10.1) as a function of the probability of visiting.

The social loss from delays in exploiting opportunities under the hierarchical form of organization are much larger than for the small world model at all the parameter settings.

10.5 Discussion

Do these models capture the relevant features of the institutional forms they are intended to represent? For example does it make sense to use the same probabilities of visiting neighbours in a firm as in a community. Workers in a firm are often required to spend time together while neighbours may barely see each other for weeks or months.

On the other hand workers in a sawmill rarely spend coffee breaks discussing how to make money for the company. In the community people do generally talk regularly to members of a small circle of friends, whether they are immediate neighbours or not. The probability of visiting is likely to be higher for the small world model, reinforcing the results above.

Do employees talk to mangers about job creation opportunities more than they talk to friends and relatives? That seems unlikely, suggesting that the kind of information we are concerned with might flow less easily within a firm. Taking this selectivity into account would reinforce our results.

It is interesting to notice that in simulations with the hierarchical models, opportunities are "discovered" at or near the central node. The fact that information is concentrated at the centre in the hierarchical model is a virtue from the point of view of management, but it also tends to provide more opportunities for those in high positions than for line workers.

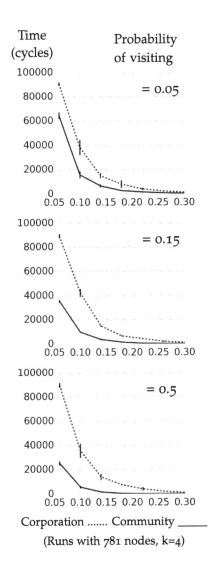

Figure 10.8: Comparing losses

Central managers may not be in the community, and may not be strongly motivated by community benefits, so our model may overestimates the innovation capacity of firms relative to community organizations. Managerial incentives encourage managers to increase profitability for the firm. Most potential innovations will not make money for the firm. There is therefore little incentive create jobs in the community, especially if the manager is not a resident. On the contrary, if there is spare capacity in the firm at the local level for such projects, there must be people who are not fully occupied, and the management should be laying them off.

Large firms have advantages. They can draw on national and international talent pools, they can afford to pay for highly trained or experienced managers and they have access to information often not available to the general public.

The internet, social media, and rising levels of education all suggest that the informational advantages of firms may be declining

130 *The Creative Potential of Community Forestry*

relative to those of community organizations, however. Information has become much cheaper to produce, store and use. The population is literate and relatively skilled with communication and computing technology. The knowledge required to manage is no longer scarce and expensive. The new technologies may allow communities to draw on high level talent and acquire information that was once restricted to central management. These trends suggest that the mode in this chapter may be underestimating the capacity of community forestry organizations.

10.6   Extensions

The model is quite simple conceptually. There are numerous extensions that might be of interest. Exploring the effect of changing the size of the networks might be revealing, and changing the degree, k, or number of links for each node, may modify results in some cases.

A number of observers (e.g., Arthur (2009)) have noted, for example, that innovation consists of combining existing components in new ways, often with relatively small adjustment. Our model has this combinatory feature, but the number of possible innovations is strictly limited in this version. Allowing for a cumulative process is likely to be revealing.

It may be of interest to see what happens if the community faced a flow of opportunities instead of a fixed set. A network of community forest networks nested in a technologically innovative society might be able to draw on a constantly growing pool of potential innovations. Alternatively, opportunities might expire over time. In either case the differences might affect the success rate.

In this model agents remember everything they learn from their neighbours. If agents forget some part of what they learn it would slow the discovery process. If only some agents are active searchers it seems likely that that too would simply slow the process. Introducing a Broken Telephone that corrupts information over time might also be interesting. Durlauf and Fafchamps (2004) point out

Conclusions **131**

that agents may compete and they may have an incentive to provide mis-information in some cases.

Since social networks are not generally static, it may be useful to explore how a community network might evolve. Linkages are maintained by individuals because they have some value and it is likely that over time the more useful links may strengthened, and less productive ones dropped. As a community gains experience in making decisions it might become more efficient at search. On the other hand, it is possible that individuals in a community might seek central positions to extract status or some form of rents, reducing the innovation efficiency. It is also possible that communities might 'learn' to create jobs. The role of economic development officer suggests that communities do invest in expanding their capacity to create jobs.

We employed a random initial distribution of ideas, but it makes sense to put more structure on the initial allocation.

10.7 Conclusions

Choosing a tenure system is really choosing a form of social capital. The network structure of industrial firms is one configuration of social capital, and the social relations within a self-governing community is another, distinctive, form of social capital. Debate about alternative tenure schemes has focussed on potential differences in sustainability and equity. Community forestry however is an institutional form with a different decision domain, an expanded set of objectives and a different social structure from the more familiar corporate form. North and Thomas (1973) argue that the fundamental explanation of comparative growth is differences in institutions. This chapter has shown that, as an institution, community forestry is likely be at least as efficient as conventional forestry in identifying and exploiting innovation opportunities at the local level.

To the best of our knowledge this is the first attempt to apply network analysis to an economic development problem of this sort.

Notes

[1] A version of this chapter was presented at the Annual conference of the Atlantic Canada Economics Association, October 23–25 2015 at Wolfville, NS, as "A network approach to the innovation potential of community forestry" by Robinson and Wright (2015).

[2] See the discussion of value-added in Chapter 4.

[3] The wild mushroom harvest in the province of British Columbia, Canada, contributes millions of dollars to local economies.

[4] Technical comment: If the rewired graph is not connected it may be rejected and the procedure repeated until a connected graph is found.

11
Coops, Worker-Managed Firms and Community Forests

The key feature of community forestry that distinguishes it from a conventional profit-maximizing industrial forestry firm is democratic management. A key question for policy makers is whether democratic management can deliver output and jobs in the forestry sector. Research on cooperatives and worker-managed firms offers some insight into the possible structure and the potential for economic success of community forestry organizations.

Such an entity would combine features of worker-managed firms, producer cooperatives, municipal enterprises, and conventional capitalist firms. The resemblance to a capitalist firm is inevitable[1] because control of production and the right to the surplus generated from the local forest is transferred to the community. These rights amount to the ownership of the forest as capital, so the community forest organization would be contributing capital to the enterprise and allocating the return on the capital.

The resemblance to a worker-managed firm or a producer cooperative is obvious because the employees will generally be members of the community and therefore owners and decision-makers. The organization may or may not be run by the local municipal government, but the concerns of a community forest organization will certainly overlap with those of the regularly constituted local government.

134 Coops, Worker-Managed Firms and Community Forests

11.1 Transitional Issues

The transition to community forestry is unlikely to be disruptive. There is no reason why a new community forest would not continue to supply wood to existing forest companies. Existing contracts would take time to unwind, and members of a community forestry organization would want to minimize disturbance to employment. Forestry companies are unlikely to care who supplies their wood as long as supplies are reliable. In the US many forestry firms are divesting themselves of forests, selling to institutional owners and relying instead on markets for their wood supply. There is no reason mills should object to community forests acting as suppliers.[2]

If the forests that are transferred to communities are economically marginal, damaged or unproductive, as has been the case in British Columbia, for example, the transfers have little immediate economic impact on supply or employment. Where wood is to be diverted to local value-added production the diversion will almost always begin slowly and even in the best case take years to affect marketed roundwood.

Legislation could be useful to ensure that transitions are not disruptive, but legislation is not likely to be needed given pre-existing contracts and the incentives for participants to cooperate.

11.2 Employment Under Community Forestry

Would community control of the forest lead to declining employment? Members of a community would clearly have an incentive to maintain their own jobs and probably to create jobs for their children and friends. Would this solidarity lead instead to featherbedding and inefficiency? Could it lead to diversification? Some guidance comes from the literature of worker-managed firms (WMFs).

The dominant model of worker-managed firm is that of Benjamin Ward (1958) in which the WMF maximizes net income per member instead of total profits. Paradoxically, in the Ward model, an income-per-worker-maximizing WMF reduces employment and output when it faces an increase in the output price. The response is not consistent with the presumed public goal.

Both theory and empirical work suggest that the WMF is likely to display more attractive behaviour. Miyazaki and Neary (1983) demonstrated that the perverse response disappears in the Ward model when the WMF provides the equivalent of unemployment insurance for laid-off members. Burdin and Dean (2012) examined the empirical literature, which shows an increase in output prices is associated with increased employment in worker-managed firms, contrary to Ward's prediction. Burdin went on to estimate a model for Uruguay that provides support for the view that WMFs are concerned with both employment and income per worker.[3]

Burdin derives a simple expression,

$$\Gamma = R^\theta L^{1-\theta},$$

that shows the relative weights that the WMF attaches to income, R, and employment, L. As θ increases, the weight that the WMF attaches to employment decreases. When $\theta = 1$ the firm will be a profit maximizer. Burdin's estimates of θ vary from 0.7021 to 0.9101 under the conservative and incorrect assumption that WMFs are no more productive than capitalist firms. If he were to assume that WMFs are more productive, estimates of θ would be smaller, implying that t WMFs would seek even higher levels of employment compared to profit maximizing firms. By extension, community forestry organizations might be expected to behave similarly.

The literature therefore provides empirical and theoretical evidence that the the objective of a community forestry organization will align with the public objective with respect to employment. This contrasts with the objective of a profit maximizing firm, which minimizes costs, and specifically the wage bill, for any level of output.

11.2.1 Output

Another policy concern is whether a community forest can achieve the same level of output as conventional firms. It is not clear that

136 Coops, Worker-Managed Firms and Community Forests

community forest organizations would want to achieve the same output profile as conventional firms, nor is it clear they should. The analogy with worker-managed firms may reassure policy-makers, however.

Dow and Putterman (2000) and Doucouliagos (1995) present evidence that labour productivity is higher on average in LMFs than in similar capitalist firms. Fakhfakh, Perotin, and Gago (2012) offer new evidence for France that labour-managed firms grow as quickly as conventional firms and are at least as efficient. Successful cooperatives, credit unions and worker-run firms do exist, and there is reason to think that they are most likely to succeed in smaller communities like the forest communities that are the focus of this book. In the USA WMFs have long been associated with the forestry industry (Hansmann, 1988; Dahl, 1957) and in Canada there have been a number of failing saw-mills taken over by workers, made profitable and sold back to private interests.

11.2.2 Security

Risk is a serious issue for workers and families in small communities. Community members are highly dependent on local harvesters and mills and vulnerable to layoffs. Unlike larger communities where housing investment can serve as a form of self-insurance, investing in a home in a forest-based community represents a failure to diversify. In single industry towns workers who invest in housing may be 'putting all their eggs in one basket'. Even without layoffs the general decline in the forest workforce means that demand for housing is weak and capital gains from housing investment are minimal. Layoffs typically result in capital losses for most members of a forest community.

Forest companies have little incentive to help diversify the local economy. Communities, however, do have an interest in stability and in diversifying products and sources of income. Diversification can be seen as a form of self-insurance that would tend to reduce the individual and social costs associated with mill closures and

Employment Under Community Forestry **137**

price fluctuations. Diversification is difficult to model and we are not aware of empirical work on this topic.

It is probably possible for a worker-managed firm to allow wages to fall when demand is low and to pay dividends out of surpluses when demand is strong. The result would be to shift variability from employment to income and to reduce the chance of bankruptcy in hard times.[4] Burdin (2014) offers evidence from Argentina that WMFs are more robust than conventional firms.

11.2.3 Human Capital

Several lines of argument lead to the conclusion that the public and government are concerned with the development of human capital. Obviously governments spend large amounts of money on behalf of the public on education. Levels of education spending are actually correlated with levels of democracy (Stasavage, 2005; Brown and Hunter, 2004), making the case difficult to argue against. It is worth adding however that measures of development, including the Human Development Index, also emphasize education levels.

Analysis and historical trends suggest that profit-maximizing firms have a more limited interest in creating human capital. Rationally they would prefer to invest only in firm-specific human capital. As worker mobility or economic uncertainty increase, investment in workers becomes less attractive. It is worth noting that human capital is produced by doing: experience is a form of human capital and human capital itself is a joint product which is not valued as highly by profit-maximizing firms as it would be by the public or a community-owned firm.

Communities, it is easily shown, have strong incentives to develop human capital and therefore would be preferred agents of the province with respect to this goal. There are at least three strong reasons to expect community forestry support for human capital formation. First, forest communities produce children, and parents want to create opportunities for their children. It is reasonable to expect that, if the power to adjust production and educational practices

138 *Coops, Worker-Managed Firms and Community Forests*

could be influenced by a community forestry organization, the organization would at least marginally adjust those practices to increase learning and opportunities for its children. Since children in these communities often wish to stay and since parents often wish children to make their homes nearby, it is likely that, if allowed, community forestry organization would adjust the education process to increase the chances that local children would be equipped for local jobs.

Since an increase in human capital is likely to increase productivity, and since net output is shared, a community would be inclined to invest in training and education of workers, and to adjust work situations to increase the skills of workers.

Finally, individual workers are more secure if they have higher levels of human capital. They will be more mobile and more able to start their own business. Profit-maximzing firms do not have this motive and demonstrate reluctance to train workers when workers cannot be tied to the firm.[5]

11.3 Exclusion

Community forestry membership is necessarily restricted to residents of a specific area, even if new residents are accepted without restriction. Durlauf and Fafchamps (2004) and Taylor (2000) have shown that clubs and networks with restricted memberships may have inequitable distributional consequences. Only those who happen to be included benefit from increased security, income and human capital. Strong social organizations may effectively penalize non-members because members of a club or network find it easier to deal with each other and, as a result, may stop dealing with non-members.

Every economically productive social organization presents similar equity issues, but the worker-managed firms and cooperatives that community forest organizations resemble have long been associated with struggles for justice and fairness. Exclusion is almost certainly less of a problem for community forestry than for the forms of economic organization that community forestry replaces.

11.4 A Final Remark on Organization

This chapter has not offered a prescription about how community forestry should be organized. It has attempted to answer the question, "Can democratic management work in the forestry sector?" The approach has been to examine the literature on worker-managed firms.

The economic literature on the subject supports a positive answer. There are many examples of successful worker-managed firms. In fact research suggests that they may be more successful, more efficient, more resilient than comparable private firms. Economic theorists have gone on to show that, not only can they succeed in the real world, they can also succeed in theory.

That is not to say that creating a successful community forestry organization is likely to be easy. Organizations are difficult to create and difficult to maintain. Most firms fail quickly, as the business press frequently points out. What the evidence shows is that, as an economic form, community forestry is as promising as the current system or any form of privatization that might be considered.

Notes

[1]Jensen and Meckling argue that it is misleading to identify the firm as an individual and speak of a "firm's objectives" when decisions come about by a more complicated process than individual decision-making. Despite this warning we will make the conventional assumption that firms maximize profits.Jensen and Meckling (1976)

[2]"The experiences in Australia and New Zealand confirmed that efficiency increased more with privatization than corporatization mainly due to sharper employment reductions and more effective marketing. However, there was no evidence of increased investment from the private sector or the emergence of entrepreneurial companies that the advocates of privatization had anticipated. Indeed, a focus on the financial aspect of plantation management led to a significant reduction in investment in reforestation and silviculture." Vertinsky and Luckert (2010).

[3]In Burdin's model the organization's objective function is, following Craig and Pencavel (1993)

$$\Gamma = \left[\left(\frac{w}{q} \right) - z \right]^{\theta} L$$

where w is real income per worker, L is the level of employment, z represent exogenous per capita inputs and q is a price index. The term in the square bracket is rent per worker, R/L.

[4]Profit maximizing firms have recourse to similar devices with profit sharing and bonuses.

[5]The objective function employed by Craig and Pencavel (1993) and Burdin and Dean (2012) should be amended to include human capital creation. Human capital terms could easily be added to the rents:

$$\Gamma = \left[\left(\frac{w}{q} \right) - z + h \right]^{\theta} L$$

where h is human capital accumulation per worker, possibly including a probability weighted sum of employment benefits to children and community members not employed by the organization. Alternatively, additions to human capital could be introduced multiplicitively:

$$\Gamma = R^{\theta} h^{\alpha} L$$

12

Community Forestry and the Professional Forester

Forestry is changing. Forest tenure and management regimes around the world are attempting to adapt to changing social and economic conditions. Hosny El Lakany (2014) , 2007 Chairman of the international Partnership for Forestry Education, summarized the general tendency, especially in the less developed countries, as follows: "Traditional forestry is giving way to forests managed increasingly by communities for their goods and services within the context of national development strategies". In 2007 participants from 29 countries at the International Workshop on Forestry Education agreed to move "towards holism" and away from industrial-based forestry education models (Ratnasingam et al., 2013). In southeast Asia, a 2004 survey showed an ongoing shift from traditional forestry towards social and community forestry, agroforestry and environmental conservation (Rudebjer and Siregar, 2004).

Kim (2014) notes in addition that "The role of the forester is changing as the forestry profession increasingly focuses on the multiple values, products and services of forests". ASuharti (2001) believes that "There has been a change of attitude among professional foresters, who mostly thought they know more in the past and had more rights over the forest. They started to realise that local people also have the right to be involved in forest management, and that

142 *Community Forestry and the Professional Forester*

community participation also has an important role in determining the success of sustainable forest management'.'

The changes, including the growth in community forestry, will inevitably open new opportunities for professional foresters. Associations of foresters will help shape community forestry through their influence on forestry education and legislation, and by their response to new forms of forest management.

> **The "practice of forestry" means the development, acquisition or application of scientific principles and practices relating to forestry, products of forested land and integrated management of forested land.**

The economic demand for foresters and their services is a 'derived' demand – it arises from the value of the forest products generated. Companies hire foresters because they want wood or pulp, not because they want foresters. Foresters are an input cost, and companies work to reduce costs. Community forestry represents a change in the valuation of the mix of products arising from the forests. The scope of forestry management is broader and the scale generally smaller.

Community forestry therefore implies changes in the demand for inputs and, potentially, the demand for the the services of foresters. That raises a sensitive question: how would community forestry affect foresters and the forestry profession? Would community forestry be good for foresters?

This is clearly a question about future demand. Experience with community forestry in Canada and the USA is simply too limited to provide an "evidence-based" answer. Even in Nepal and Indonesia, developing countries that are deeply committed to community forestry, the systems have not reached maturity and the role of professional foresters is still evolving.

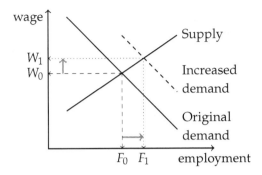

Figure 12.1: Supply and demand for foresters

Theory does provide some guidance, however. The question we want to answer is, "If community forestry expands how will it affect the demand for professional foresters?" This is what economists call a problem in comparative statics. The 'method of comparative statics' is taught in any first-year economic class. The typical example begins with a supply and demand graph like Figure 12.1 that describes an initial, 'static' situation. Students are then asked to consider the effect of an *'exogenous shock'*. An exogenous shock is just any change coming from outside of the market that might affect supply or demand.

In our case we have the current supply and demand for professional foresters and the exogenous shock is the growth of community forestry. If community forestry simply increased the demand for foresters, the effect would be to move the demand curve to the right, resulting in a larger number employed, F_1 and a higher wage, W_1 as Figure 12.1 shows.

12.1 Declining Demand for Professional Foresters

The story is not quite as simple as Figure 12.1 suggests. Although global employment in forestry has not changed much over the last two decades, employment in the high labour-productivity boreal

Table 12.1: Aspects of the practice of forestry

1. the inventory, classification, appraisal and evaluation of forests and forested land,
   - Timber inventories and the economic valuation of timber
   - Ecological and site classification of forested lands
   - Audits (forest management performance and environmental protection)
2. the development and implementation of programmes for harvesting and renewal of forests and forested land,
   - Harvest plans and block layouts
   - Silviculture/regeneration plans or surveys
   - Pre- and post-harvest assessments or prescriptions
   - Supervising regeneration and harvest programmes
   - Free-to-grow sign off
   - Cone provenance registration
   - Forest Road Design and Planning
   - Annual operating plan
   - Preliminary and general management plans
3. the conservation, reclamation, improvement or protection of forests, forested land or forest soils for forestry purposes,
   - Fire Protection (fire management)
   - Prescribed burn plan
   - Forest Health (herbicide/pesticide programmes, forest insect and disease surveys)
   - Erosion and road stabilization control programmes
4. the preparation of forest resource management plans,
   - AAC calculations
   - Timber Growth and Yield Curve Development
   - Forest growth models
   - Timber supply analysis
   - Forest management planning
5. the development of integrated resource management plans and administration of forested land
   - Involvement in the planning process with other professionals and the public in the development of integrated forest management plans
   - Preparation and implementation of regulations and policies pertinent to forest resource management and protection
6. teaching forestry at a college, technical institute or university
7. conducting of research activities related to forestry.

From Section 1(1)(u) of the Alberta Regulated Forestry Profession Act

forests has been declining (Whiteman, Wickramasinghe, and Piña, 2015). Furthermore, demand for the professional foresters has been declining. In 2004 C.T.S. Nair, Chief of the Forest Economics Service, of the FAO Forestry Department, listed a series of changes that affect the prospects for professional foresters (Nair, 2004):

- the role of the public sector in forest management has been increasingly assumed by the private sector. Professional foresters have been predominantly employed in the public sector;
- large multinational corporations increasingly dominate production, especially in the pulp and paper sector;[1]
- forest plantations, which require higher initial labour inputs but simplify production, provide an increasing share of the world wood supply;
- decentralization and devolution of administration to local bodies and the declining importance of hierarchical forestry administrations seem to be accelerating;
- most increases in production in the primary sectors, including forestry, will be achieved through productivity-enhancing technologies that are unlikely to be accompanied by increased employment, even of professionals;
- emphasis on community participation and transfer (including restoration) of ownership and management to local communities and individuals;
- increasing activity by and recognition of non-governmental organizations in advocacy and support to local communities.

Based on these trends, Nair, who could be described as Chief Forester to the world when he made these observations in 2004, concluded that job opportunities for professional foresters are unlikely to expand.

Costa Rica, Guatemala and Nicaragua were showing signs of saturation in the market for professional foresters in 2004 (Rodríguez, 2004). In Canada, the Council of Forest Ministers in 2004 observed declining employment for foresters. The total number would continue to decline, although a wave of retirements was expected to increase the demand for new foresters. In the USA, employment of conservation scientists and foresters was projected to grow at 3

146 *Community Forestry and the Professional Forester*

percent from 2012 to 2022, significantly below the average of 11% for all occupations (BLS, 2015).

Recent large-scale sales of forestlands by industry have resulted in a loss of jobs in the traditional forest industry while creating limited opportunities with timber investment management organizations and real estate investment trusts. The category of self-employed foresters, who advise private landowners on a contract basis, is likely to see modest growth. Overall, however, demand for professional foresters appears to be declining.

12.2   *The Declining Attractiveness of Forestry*

The supply of foresters responds to demand. A number of studies in recent years have drawn attention to the declining state of professional forestry education,[2] both in developing and developed countries. Symptoms of this decline include a significant reduction in funding for educational institutions, low student enrolment rates (van Lierop, 2003), and an inability to attract the most talented students (Nair, 2004).

In Africa, forestry education was declining in terms of both relevance and quality (Hamid, 2004). In Canada, the Council of Forest Ministers in 2004 noted declining enrolment in forestry schools and undertook a study of demand. In Great Britain and Germany there was a steady decline in numbers entering degree programmes in forestry in established universities over the decade 1992 to 2001 (Miller, 2004). Since peaking at over 3,000 in the 1998/99 academic year, undergraduate enrolment in Canadian university forestry programmes has declined by nearly 46%. In British Columbia enrolment in general forestry programmes (e.g., professional foresters) has trended downwards since 2006–07, and enrolment in bachelor's programmes actually dropped to zero in 2009/10, where it remained for at least three years (Insight and Associates, 2013).

In terms of Figure 12.1, both supply and demand curves are shifting to the left independent of any move toward community forestry. The effect on wages is ambiguous: if supply shrinks more slowly than demand, wages will tend to fall.

12.3 More Comparative Statics

Since community forestry has only a tiny share of the forests of most developed countries the effect will certainly be small compared to the major trends. We can say a bit more, however. First, community forestry withdraws land from industrial forestry. That has the effect of reducing demand from the industrial sector while increasing demand from the smaller community forestry sector. The crucial question, then, is whether community forestry uses more or fewer foresters per unit of land.

The question cannot be answered easily. Since community forests tend to be small relative to industrial tenures, they are likely to require more foresters overall. It is also likely that community forests will be more intensively managed and managed for more products than industrial forests which will increase the demand for the skills of professional foresters. If that is the case, there will be an increase in demand for forestry skills and knowledge. On the other hand, small-scale production employs fewer professional foresters than industrial forestry relative to the amounts of wood produced. Moreover, employment in community-managed initiatives may not be attractive in terms of remuneration and other benefits (Nair, 2004). With democratization and increased public participation, more of the knowledge and skills are likely to come from knowledgeable non-professionals. There is some evidence that in developing countries the move toward community forestry is accompanied by a reduction in the services of professional foresters in the public sector.

The overall effect that expanding community forestry will have on the employment of forestry professionals is uncertain. In boreal forests, where management investment is relatively low and appears to be declining it seems likely that the effect will be positive because of the increased intensity of management. The effects are almost certain to be small.

12.4 Job Qualilty

Community forestry will have an effect on the quality of work for professional foresters. In general, community forest members are interested in a wider variety of products than most forestry firms, a wider set of environmental issues, and more specific features in their environment. The forester for a community forest is likely to deal with a greater variety of problems and a more granular and detailed set of tasks. In addition the forester will work more directly with community members and engage in more intensive public education. All of these features suggest that community forestry will be make the profession more interesting, at least for some professional foresters.

On the other hand, most foresters in developed countries have been employed by either industry or government. Jobs with community forests are likely to pay less than public sector or industry jobs.

12.5 Conclusions

For those who are currently employed, community forestry is likely to have very little direct effect. For those entering the profession, and perhaps for those retiring, it will offer new kinds of opportunities. There will also be legislative and organizational innovations that will affect a growing number of foresters.

The community forestry sector will almost inevitably expand. To succeed, communities will need the knowledge and the skills of professional foresters. Based on the overview in this chapter, professional associations of foresters have a corporate interest in promoting community-based forestry and in participating in shaping its development.

Notes

[1] In Canada forestry companies have argued successfully for larger management units and less frequent revisions to the forestry plans. Although not stated explicitly, the goal is to reduce expenditure on the services of professional foresters. The proposals could cut demand for foresters by a factor of four: half as many management units reporting half as often.

[2] Traditionally forestry education has largely concentrated on the supply side of the equation, assuming a continued upward trend in the demand for wood and wood products and thus the need to produce more forestry professionals and technicians (Nair, 2004).

13
Conclusions and Policy Advice

The analysis in this book makes the case that community forestry would be at least as productive and innovative as the current industrial regimes. Benner, Lertzman, and Pinkerton (2014) argue that community forests as a group have performed better than major industrial tenures in delivering local benefits If this is the case, there is no economic reason for governments to continue to discriminate in favour of the dominant corporate/industrial model.[1] On the contrary, there are good reasons to facilitate the emergence of a strong community forestry sector.

This chapter looks at the policy challenges raised by any attempt to develop a vigorous community forestry sector. The central concerns are with rights and revenue allocation, responsibilities, fairness, succession, and accountability. These concerns are brought to questions such as: Should there be state or province-level guidelines? How much local autonomy should be permitted? What happens if a community declines or if a new community develops in the region? Can a community negotiate a forest lease that is equivalent to the leases currently offered by the state? Can community forest lease woodlots to individuals or families?[2] Should the state retain a share of the income or continue to collect stumpage fees? What level of government is responsible for fire suppression and insect control?

152 *Conclusions and Policy Advice*

Who pays for silviculture research? Should community members be allowed to receive a dividend, as members would in a coop? What can be used as collateral for loans? What provision should be made for access by non-members? Does the state or province contribute to the cost of access roads? How can compliance costs be minimized?

This mass of questions can be addressed, it turns out, with just a few guiding principles. While these principles don't by themselves solve the thorny issues of fairness and rights allocation, they have a long track record of allowing for relatively effective and equitable governance of common property resources.

13.1   Design Principles for Community Forestry

Governments considering tenure reform do not have to invent a community-friendly system from scratch. Ostrom (1990) and Ostrom (1995), and others, demonstrate that communities have successfully managed resources in the past and continue to do so in many places. There is also extensive research on the factors that contribute to the success of community-based resource management.

Ostrom (1990) first proposed a set of design principles for community-based natural resource management. Twenty years later, using the results of over 100 studies, Cox, Arnold, and Tomás (2010) updated the list, and their list is paraphrased below. Items one to four have been discussed in Chapters 1 and 3. They are more or less implicit in the definition of community forestry used in this study. The other five items have to do with the internal workings and incentive structures of community forest organizations.

1. Clear and locally understood boundaries between legitimate users and non-users are present.[3]
2. Clear socially and environmentally appropriate territorial boundaries.
3. Autonomy: government recognition of the rights of local users to make and enforce their own rules.
4. Inclusive democracy.[4]

Design Principles for Community Forestry 153

5. A distribution of costs that is proportional to the distribution of benefits.
6. Monitoring by the users. (The community has ways to determine the condition of the resource and who is taking what.)
7. Graduated Sanctions: sanctions for rule violations start very low but become stronger if a user repeatedly violates a rule.
8. Low-cost, local conflict-resolution mechanisms.
9. Nested Enterprises: when a common-pool resource is closely connected to a larger social-ecological system, governance activities are organized in multiple nested layers.

Additional research summarized by Singh, Pandey, and Prakash (2011) identified the crucial conditions for success: "local monitoring and enforcement of locally made rules is now emerging as one of the most important determinants of sustainable governance of forests and protected areas".[5] Item 3, autonomy is necessary for locally made rules. Items six to eight are conditions for effective monitoring and enforcement. Taken together, the design principles and subsequent research can be summarized as recommending effective devolution combined with the creation or development of local governance institutions.

The most important principle for effective governance are, first, clear and secure tenure,[6] second, the power to make and enforce rules for the local forests, and third, the right to appropriate earnings generated from the forest.

Most of the studies cited were based on variants of community forestry in developing nations that fall short of the clear devolution of powers and secure effective ownership called for in this study. In the developed world secure tenure rights are the norm, but communities do not have the rights, either to access resources or to appropriate income. Any policy for community forestry must begin here.

154 *Conclusions and Policy Advice*

13.2 *Assigning Rights*

Table 13.1 lists six dimensions of forest tenure rights and indicates the nature of the rights that would be assigned to a community forest organization under a community forest regime. The first two simply define a forest and a community. Comprehensiveness, permanence and security of tenure are necessary for economic efficiency. Economic theory predicts that insecure ownership will induce shorter rotation periods on forests cut for timber. Deacon (1999) observes that "short rotations, in turn, can cause forest land to degenerate into wasteland".

The principle restriction on the rights of community in the ideal case is that the forest itself cannot be sold. That does not prevent a community from entering into contracts to deliver wood in the future, or using the expected stream of revenue from the forest as security in a financial transaction.

13.3 *Equity and Community Forestry*

At first glance assigning control and returns to local communities may appear to privilege a local clique at the expense of the larger community. Why should any small group be given special access to resource rents that rightly belong to the entire state? Setting aside the fact that that is precisely what the current system does in most countries, it is doubtful that significant resource rents are generated any longer in the boreal forest. In Ontario, for instance, in 2009/10 most of the fees collected from harvest companies were returned for forest maintenance. The Government of Ontario received a total of approximately $68 million from timber sales, of which approximately $50.8 million went directly to funds designated for the maintenance and renewal of the forest, and for work associated with ensuring the future of the forest. The remaining $17 million accruing to general revenue was negligible compared to annual fire control costs over the 90 million hectares of crown forests. The Ministry of Natural resources provided approximately $75 million for road construction

Table 13.1: Six features of the ideal community forestry tenure

	Rights dimension	Description	Ideal
1	allotment type	whether the tenure is area- or volume-based	area
2	exclusiveness	who may be excluded from enjoying a given property right	non-residents
3	comprehensiveness	what powers over which resources and what benefits maybe appropriated	comprehensive
4	duration and renewability	the period of time for which these rights can be exercised and whether they can be renewed	permanent
5	security	the degree of confidence that the right will not be attenuated or cancelled	complete
6	transferability	can these rights be transferred and what conditions are imposed on these transfers	none

and maintenance activities (OMNR, 2009). Total 2007/08 fire control expenditures, for example, were $135 million according to the 2006 Auditor's Annual Report (Auditor General, 2006 p 391).

If there are still rents for producers and they were transferred to the community, there would no longer be non-resident owners. The province would capture a larger share of the rents though income and other taxes on the workers in the community than it captures from the forest companies.

13.4 Negotiating a Transition

Legislators involved in tenure reform would be well advised not to treat community forestry as a model that can be easily grafted on to the legislative framework designed to promote corporate forestry.[7] Chapter 6 showed that community forestry is a more

156 *Conclusions and Policy Advice*

general economic form than conventional industrial tenures: the benefits of conventional tenure are available within a community forestry framework. The converse is not true.

As Roberts and Gautam (2003) pointed out, it is important to resolve any conflicting claims on resources such as timber industry versus environmental interests and indigenous claims and cultural concerns in any reallocation of forest resources: "Only then can the local institutions be developed for community input into forest management." It is far from trivial to settle these conflicting claims. Furthermore, it is not enough to authorize a processes of decentralization and democratization, because any reallocation of authority will be contested. Those who stand to lose from decentralization can be expected to defend their authority and access to resources as well as they can (Poteete and Ribot, 2010).

The project is further complicated because the goal is not to create legislation that allows communities to act as forest companies.[8] The goal is to enable communities to act as governments. Vesting real power in communities requires existing authorities to give us some of their own power.

Once the community has the power to act as a company, it can if it desires, act like a company, create a company to manage forests or contract with private suppliers for management services. Attempts to limit the power of the community will reduce the effectiveness of reforms. As Buchy and Race (2001) point out, "the greater the control by 'outsiders' (e.g. those outside the local community), the less local communities tend to be involved at critical stages of decision making".

Governments and their bureaucracies may prefer to effect the transfer by decree, administrative order or permit, rather than through legislation. These administrative arrangements are likely to be limited, with important commercial products like timber excluded, and they can later be withdrawn or restricted by later decree (Agrawal and Ribot, 1999). Even if rights are vested through legislation they may not be upheld by law. This undermines the potential of community forestry.

Negotiating a Transition **157**

While implementing a legislative regime supportive of community forestry is challenging, it has benefits. As argued in this book, community forestry has the potential to be more economically efficient, equitable, and ecologically sound than what it replaces. Furthermore, as an extension of democratic governance, community forestry relieves the central authority of responsibility for management and enforcement. It does that by creating new capacity for self-governance and for economic production at the community level. In doing so, it expands the capacity of society overall.

158 *Notes*

Notes

[1]"Community forestry still has considerable potential for success when state and sub-national agencies have the political will to work with local communities, providing financial subsidy, technical assistance, and degrees of accountability, transparency and (local) autonomy." Dressler, McDermott, and Schusser (n.d.)

[2] "As methods for aggregating the preferences of a group of patrons, such collective choice mechanisms often involve substantial costs in comparison to market contracting. Little attention has been devoted to these costs in the literature on corporate control and the economics of organizational form. Nevertheless, they appear to be crucial in determining the efficiency of alternative assignments of ownership". Hansmann (1988))=

[3]"We also find that strong autonomy of rule-making at the local level (and not the government-imposed rules) is the key predictor of both better forests and yield of goods and services to support livelihoods of local people." Singh, Pandey, and Prakash (2011)

[4]"We conclude that the presumed benefits of decentralization become available to local populations only when empowered local actors are downwardly accountable." (Agrawal and Ribot, 1999)

[5]"In modern community-based forest management systems, the communities are the nuclei of the management system rather than being subordinate to, for example, the state." Castén (2005)

[6]"Among the constraints to success noted by a high proportion of researchers are insecure property rights and a lack of infrastructure from which to build capacity to act". Glasmeier and Farrigan (2005)

[7]"Indeed, we can view business corporation statutes as simply specialized versions of the more general cooperative corporation statutes. In principle, there is no need to have separate business corporation statutes at all; business corporations could just as well be organized under a well-drafted general cooperative corporation statute." (Hansmann, 1988)

[8]"To be effective, empowerment needs not only to establish or recognize their rights of ownership or use, but also to enable the recipients to exercise their authority and rights." (Arnold, 2001)

Appendices

A

A Brief Introduction to Traditional Forestry Economics

Forest economics is the application of economic principles to a range of subjects extending from management of forest resources through the processing, marketing and consumption of forest products. According to Sills and Abt (2003),"Traditional forest economics is concerned with producers who are assumed to maximize profits subject to production technology and exogenous prices". C.T.S Nair, Chief of the Forest Economics Service, of the UN's Food and Agriculture Organization Forestry Department, has written that "Historically most of the forestry knowledge system – which includes research, education, training and extension – has been largely geared to the needs of industrial forestry. In most countries forestry departments were established almost entirely to protect forests and to secure industrial wood supplies to meet domestic or external demand."

This appendix introduces what is sometimes called the bioeconomics of forestry. It is an approach that combines knowledge of how a biological stock changes through time with the modern economic approach to optimization. The first question in the bioeconomics of forestry is simply how long to let your trees grow.

> "The oldest traceable research in natural resource economics is arguably an analysis of a forest rotation, or the time at which a forest owner should harvest." Amacher, Ollikainen, and Koskela (2009) p3.

162 *A Brief Introduction to Traditional Forestry Economics*

There are several factors that distinguish forest economics as a separate applied field of economics. First, the diversity of forest landowners, both by groups (public, and private industrial and nonindustrial) and within groups, leads to a diversity of preferences, expectations, and constraints. Second, the long time frames involved in forest production give rise to the classical problem of choosing optimal rotation lengths, capital budgeting, and modern financial analysis. A third complicating factor is that forests jointly produce multiple outputs, some extracted and some valued in situ, some traded in the market and some not, and some accruing to forest owners and some to the public. Those not traded in the market, whether consumed by landowners or by the public, have no market price signals to predict behaviour or guide allocation. Fourth, the immobility of forests lends greater importance to the issue of market power and to travel costs as necessary inputs to forest use.

Sills and Abt, 2003. *Forests in a Market Economy*

A.1 *A Biological and Economic Model of Forest Growth*

Trees are a renewable. Unlike fish they are tied to land for which property rights are easily assigned and fairly easily defended. The natural comparison then is with other forms of agriculture. What differs? First, the length of the period between harvests. Second, forests initially come with a basic stock of resource, unlike general

A Biological and Economic Model of Forest Growth **163**

agricultural land, which must be broken and planted before it can be harvested. There is a windfall profit in the first harvest.

After a harvest it takes a long time to grow another stock of trees. The problem we want to solve is how long to wait before harvesting the new stock of trees. Time is the choice variable and the problem is to find the optimal rotation period.

Foresters imagine a growth function that describes how much wood has been produced in a given stand T years after the the forest was planted. This function, $f(T)$, is the foundation of the analysis that follows. $f(T)$ is short for $f(s, L; T)$, where L is labour input at the beginning of one planting cycle and s is the land used throughout that complete cycle. A basic analysis focusses on choosing T,

Table A.1: Content of an introductory course in forestry economics

- Introduction to Economics and Forest Economics
- The Economic Importance of Forests
- Wood Recovery Considerations in Logging
- The Value of a Cubic Metre of Wood
- Can a Value be Assigned to Non-Timber Forest Products?
- What is the value of an area of forest land for timber production?
- The Financial Analysis of Silvicultural Operations
- How should the use of forestland be organized to maximize net benefits to the public?
- Property Rights and the Forest Tenure System

Based on Forestry 319, Principles of Forestry Economics, UBC, 2013

164 A Brief Introduction to Traditional Forestry Economics

although many other management decisions affect the output as well. These include stocking density when the forest is replanted after each harvest, pruning, thinning, fertilization.[1]

In the usual mathematical treatment, the rate of growth in any year, called the annual increment (AI) or the current annual increment (CAI), is represented by the derivative, or slope of $f(T)$, $f'(T)$. The mean annual increment (MAI) of average growth rate is written $\frac{f(T)}{T}$. A third concept, sometimes called the proportional annual increment, PAI, $\frac{f'(T)}{f(T)}$ is the rate of growth of a unit of wood. It is the rate of return on standing trees.

Economists generally prefer to speak in value-terms. The *value* of wood in a stand is the price of the wood times the quantity, $V(t) =$

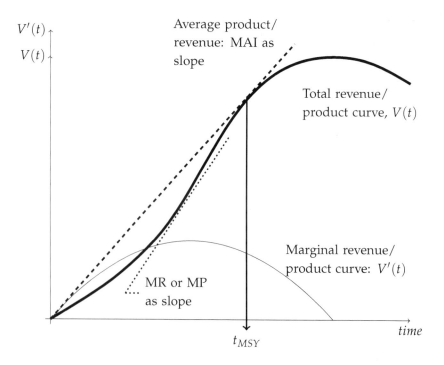

Figure A.1: Marginal and total product curves for a timber stand

$pf(t)$. If we let $p = 1$, the amount of wood and the amount of value are the same: $V(t) = f(t)$. The same curve can represent the revenue function and the growth function. Changing the price simply scales the curve up or down.

$V(t)$ is shown by the the heavy solid line in Figure A.1. The Mean Annual Increment (MAI) is the average value produced per unit of time before harvest. In the graph, it is the height of the curve at any point, $V(t)$, divided by the length of the rotation, t. In other words it is just the slope of the dashed line from the origin to any point on the lines, $V(t)/t$.

$V(t)$ has to level off completely when insects, fire and decay just balance the growth of new timber. It may then decline as decay and other damage increases.

The slope of the line $V(t)$ at any time shows the value of wood added in a given year. We designate the rate of growth by $V'(t)$ (Vee

Table A.2: Some determinants of the value of a tree

1. Stem diameter: With increasing stem diameter, logging and manufacturing costs decrease, whereas lumber volume recovery and grade yield increase significantly.
2. Stem form or defects: May considerably reduce lumber volume recovery and quality.
3. Stem taper: Decreases with denser planting. It has the greatest influence on the value of a tree of a particular diameter. Recovery decreases significantly with increasing stem taper.
4. Tree age.

Jozsa and Middleton (1994) and Zhang (2003)

prime). This is the value of the Annual Increment. It can also be called the marginal revenue. The $V'(t)$ curve starts at zero height because when there are no trees there is no growth. It rises because as we get more trees there is more biomass to grow. It peaks where the slope of $V(t)$ is steepest, then falls to zero when the forest is completely mature.[2]

Figure A.1 summarizes the biology of the forest in value terms. Students of microeconomics will notice that the figure is very like the standard total product curve for a firm with increasing returns at the beginning (rising slope) and decreasing returns (decreasing slope) later on.

A.2   A Candidate Solution: Maximum Sustainable Yield

The next step is to figure out how long to let the forest grow.

One possible goal for a land owner would be to maximize the amount of wood that we take from a stand of trees. This goal makes sense, although it is not what an economist would do. Let's see where this leads us using the model in Figure A.1.

Maximizing total output means we need to find the rotation period that gives us the highest *average* rate of growth, $V(t)/t$, or **Maximum Sustainable Yield** (MSY). Differentiating using the quotient rule we get,

$$\frac{\partial \frac{V(t)/t}{t}}{\partial t} = \frac{V'(t)}{t} - \frac{V(t)}{t^2}$$

Setting this equal to zero we get an extremum when

$$V'(t_c) = \frac{V(t_c)}{t_c}$$

This occurs where the dashed line from the origin to the total revenue cure is steepest. That point is shown in Figure A.1.

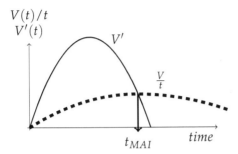

Figure A.2: Maximum mean annual increment

A.2.1 MSY is where CAI = MAI

There is a closely related way to look at the problem that is economically interesting. In Figure A.2 we have copied a taller version of the marginal value curve from Figure A.1. This is proportional to the Current Annual Increment (CAI) described above. The higher, thin line in Figure A.2 is the same as the thin $V'(t)$ line in Figure A.1. The lower thick dashed line is a new curve representing the average revenue generated $\frac{V(t)}{t}$. This is proportional to the Mean annual Increment (MAI).

Whenever the current increment is larger than the average increment, the average must be rising, and when the marginal increment is smaller than the average the average must be falling. It follows that the maximum of the MAI must occurs where MAI=CAI.

From the figures it is easy to see that the Maximum Sustainable Yield occurs where the average growth rate is equal to the marginal growth rate. (In Figure A.1 that happens where the dotted and dashed lines have the same slope.) Choosing the time to harvest that yields the highest average growth of value, then replanting and repeating the cycle maximizes the Mean Annual Increment or MAI.

The rotation age which maximizes the MAI or long-run average value yield is known as the **culmination age**.

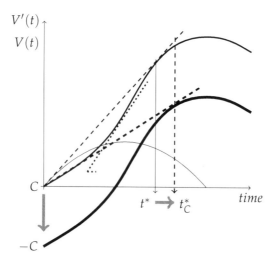

Figure A.3: Maximizing net revenue

A.2.2 The Cost of Harvesting

Introducing a harvest cost, C is simple: we maximize average *net* revenue. Differentiating

$$\frac{\partial \frac{V(T)-C}{T}}{\partial t} = \frac{V'(t)}{t} - \frac{V(t)-C}{t^2}$$

which, when set equal to zero, gives us

$$V'(T) = \frac{V(T)-C}{T} = \frac{V(T)}{T} - \frac{C}{T}$$

Average net revenue is then negative for the first period of any rotation. Graphically, subtracting C from V shifts the V curve downward, reducing the slope of the dashed line in Figure A.3, and resulting in a longer rotation.

According to Reed, "The traditional objective of forestry management has been to obtain a normal forest, containing equal areas in each age class up to the culmination age, so that if each stand is harvested at the culmination age, an even-flow of timber volume, proportional to the maximum MAl, will be extracted from the forest." With harvest costs, the rotation period should actually be longer to reduce the average harvest and planting costs. Maximizing the Mean Annual Increment of wood is a goal based entirely on biological criteria. Maximizing the Mean annual increase in net revenue is an economic goal.

Contents of a textbook in forestry economics

- Forestry's Economic Perspective
- Economic Efficiency and Market Failures in Forestry
- Timber Supply, Demand, and Pricing
- Unpriced Forest Values
- Land Allocation and Multiple Use
- Valuation over Time and Investment Criteria
- The Optimum Forest Rotation
- Regulating Harvests over Time
- Property Rights and Tenure Systems
- Taxes and Other Charges
- Developments in Forestry Economics

From Peter H. Pearse *Introduction to Forestry Economics* (Pearse, 1990)

170 *A Brief Introduction to Traditional Forestry Economics*

A.2.3 *Fire*

Reed and Errico (1986) have shown that even low rates of fire can cause considerable reductions in long-run average volume yield and in land-expectation value, and they point out that the benefits of reforestation and other silvicultural treatments need to be re-evaluated when there is a risk of fire present.

It is easy to modify the graph to take into account the risk of fire. The longer we wait to harvest, the greater the chance that the forest will burn and the larger the economic loss. If climate warming continues, increasing the chance of fires, as it is expected to do, rotation periods should be shortened.

A.3 *Faustmann Model*

The best known model in forestry economics also deals with the length of the period between harvests. The **Faustmann model** is named for German forester Martin Faustmann (1822–1876). Faustmann's 1849 seminal article "Calculation of the Value which Forest Land and Immature Stands Possess for Forestry" introduced an approach to maximizing the value of forest lands. Updated versions of his model form the core of modern forestry economics.

Faustmann pointed out in 1849 that the value of forest land as an investment is the present value of the sequence of harvests from the land, discounted at the appropriate rate. It makes sense to choose a rotation period that maximizes the *value* of the forest land rather than the quantity of wood produced. This is an economic goal, while MSY is actually not an economic goal at all: it simply identifies a feature of the growth function. MSY is a biological criterion, not an economic one.[3] The two criteria differ because the revenue from future harvests is *discounted*. Maximizing the MAI treats wood harvested in 1000 years as if it was as valuable to the owner as wood harvested today. If the owner has a time preference – if she prefers money today to money tomorrow – she will discount the future harvests, and her rotation period should take that into account. Some

Faustmann Model **171**

forest economists (e.g Duerr, Fedkiw and Guttenburg, 1956) have used the term 'financial maturity' to indicate the age at which a stand should be cut from an economic point of view.

Faustmann's 1849 formula gives the present value of the income stream for a known forest rotation period. Faustmann didn't try to find the optimal rotation period. The solution to the problem of maximizing the present value by choosing the length of rotations was published by Bertil Ohlin in 1921 (translated as Ohlin (1995)), and the solution became known as the Faustmann-Ohlin theorem, although other German foresters were aware of the correct solution in 1860.

If $f(T)$ is the stock of timber at time T, p is the price of timber, and $C(T)$ is the cost of harvesting, then $V(T) = pf(T) - C(T)$ is the net value of forest at time T, when it is cut. The net present value of the harvest if we cut it at time T is

$$PV = [pf(T) - C(T)]e^{-rT}$$

If we cut again after each T, the present value of the forest with the rotation plan is the sum of discounted values,

$$PV = \sum_{j=1}^{\infty} V(T)e^{-rT}$$
$$= V(T)]e^{-rT}(1 + e^{-rT} + e^{-2rT} + \cdots) \qquad (A.1)$$
$$= \frac{V(T)}{e^{rT} - 1}$$

This can be maximized with respect to T by setting the derivative with respect to T to zero:

$$\frac{\partial PV}{\partial T} = \frac{1}{e^{rT} - 1}V'(T) - \frac{1}{(e^{rT} - 1)^2}rV(T) = 0$$

The result is known as the Faustmann equation:

$$V'(T) = \frac{r}{1 - e^{-rT}}V(T)$$

172 *A Brief Introduction to Traditional Forestry Economics*

or

$$(1 - e^{-rT})\frac{V'(T)}{V(T)} = r \qquad\qquad (A.2)$$

The Faustmann equation is just the necessary condition for maximizing present value. It says the discounted rate of return on not harvesting immediately has to equal the market rate of interest. We can think of the harvest decision as a portfolio choice: Should I take my money out of forest and put it in the bank to collect r, or should I wait for one more period and benefit from the growth of the trees?

On the left, $V'(T)$ is the net value of the new wood that would grow in any period if we lengthen each rotation slightly. $\frac{V'(T)}{V(T)}$ is the rate of return on the capital value of the wood in the harvest. With constant prices and no costs of harvest or planting it turns out to be the biological rate of return for the forest. Since we have to wait longer for all the future harvests, each gain is discounted by $1 - e^{-rT}$.

Equation **??** provides an important result. The higher the interest rate the higher $V'(T)$ has to be. But $V'(T)$ depends on the rate of growth, which is falling as T increases, so to balance a rising interest rate it is necessary to reduce the rotation period. Relative to the rotation period for Maximum Sustainable Yield, the economically optimal rotation period is shorter..

The Faustman rule illustrates a general principle: faced with harvesting now or later, we simply ask whether we get a larger return by harvesting and investing the money or by waiting. The principle would hold if we included price changes, benefits from mushrooms and caribou, or tourism revenues, although the arithmetic would be more complicated.

Most versions of the Faustmann harvest decision approach ignore annual timber price fluctuations and prescribes harvest on the basis of expected prices. Brazee and Mendelsohn (1988) recognized the volatility of timber prices from year to year, and incorporated a stochastic timber price into their work. They concluded that a harvest policy derived form a variable-price model significantly increases the present value of expected returns over the simple Faustmann model.

A.3.1 The Heroic Assumptions Needed for the Faustmann Model

Samuelson (1976) pointed out that certain "heroic assumptions" must be made if we want a simple solution to the Faustmann rotation problem These include:

1. fixed (or at least known) future lumber prices and costs;
2. fixed (or known) future interest rates;
3. identical (or known) biological growth characteristics for every stand established on the site;
4. the assumption of a perfect market in forest land (or if a government owns public lands that it rents them at rates determined in a perfect market, and that it conducts its own forestry operations to earn the maximum rent using the market rate of interest).

To these William Reed (1985) added:

5. that a more or less instantaneous harvest at the selected rotation age can be accomplished in spite of the location of the site relative to roads and established logging operations;
6. that externalities such as the recreational value of forest land, its usefulness for wildlife habitat, flood prevention, oxygen production, etc. can all be safely ignored;
7. that one can be certain that catastrophes such as fire or pest infestation will not destroy a stand;
8. that a perfect capital market exists in which unrestricted amounts can be loaned or borrowed at the same interest rate.

And a current generation would insist on adding that:

9. climate and environmental conditions remain constant.

Reed notes that "When one recognizes that rotation lengths of 60 to 100 years are not uncommon in forestry operations, one realizes that these assumptions are, indeed, truly heroic."

"Heroic assumptions" allow us to simplify to the point where we can understand the basic features of a model. It is important to remember that the simple special case we understand may not describe the world we actually live in as well as we might like.

174 *A Brief Introduction to Traditional Forestry Economics*

A.3.2 *The Cost of Harvesting*

The analysis above hides the cost term. We are really interested in maximizing the *net* value of our forest, which is the present value of *all* the net benefits from owning it *minus* any costs. $V(T) = p(T)f(T) - C(T)$. The price in this case is the price relative to the general price level. If the general price level changes exactly as much as the price of timber there it will have no effect.[4]

Dropping the (T) from all terms, we can write $V'(T) = pf' + p'f - C'$. This term can be substituted into Equation **??** to get

$$(1 - e^{-rT}) \frac{pf' + p'f - C'}{pf - C} = r \tag{A.3}$$

If cost doesn't change as trees get bigger, $C' = 0$. Bigger trees take longer to cut down and are heavier to move, but there are probably fewer of them and trucks can be loaded more quickly. This is a less heroic simplification than the ones we have already accepted!

If prices don't change, $p' = 0$. If prices are expected to change *relative to the general price level*, the owner should consider the growth in the price of the forest as well as the growth of the forest.

The key to notice here is the general structure. The new term when we introduce prices is $\dot{p}/p$, the rate of change of prices. It tells us that we want to take into account the growth rate, $\dot{H}$, the interest rate AND the growth of value due to price changes when we make our investment decision about leaving or cutting the stock.

A.4 *The Hartman Model*

What if the trees and fish are valuable for some reason other than the price we can sell them for? Trees might fix carbon and free oxygen, provide campsites, and serve as nesting areas for birds (Skutsch, 2004). These are benefits that will be lost if the stock of standing trees is reduced. Costs or benefits that accrue to anyone other than the decision-maker are called 'external' costs or benefit.[5] Externalities that result from reducing the stock of trees do not normally appear on the books of the harvesting company. Richard Hartman (1976) generalized the Faustmann-Ohlin rule to include such tradeoffs between timber returns and other outputs such as amenities and ecosystem services.

> The basic conclusion of this analysis is that the presence of recreational or other services provided by a standing forest may well have a very important impact on when or whether a forest should be harvested. Those models which consider only the timber value of a forest are likely to provide incorrect information in the many cases where a standing forest provides a significant flow of valuable services.

If, in addition to the growth of the trees and any price-appreciation, there are other benefits from not cutting they appear on the left side of Equation A.3. With extra benefits on the left hand side the owner should delay the harvest until the growth rate of timber falls far enough to balance the interest rate on the right. There have been literally several hundreds of articles written using this framework, and applications continue to show up in the literature even today. Most forestry economics textbooks now include a treatment of the Hartman model.

A.4.1 Forest-level Management

Faustmann models and their derivatives, like the Hartman model, can be directly applied only to problems where the forest is a single even-aged stand of trees. Most management units are not at the stand level. The objective at the forest level is usually to provide a fairly even and large flow of timber from the management unit. Forestry theory has developed the ideal of a "normal forest". consisting of equal areas. The oldest class is harvested each year and replaced (planted) with the youngest (Reed, 1985; Amacher, Ollikainen, and Koskela, 2009).

If the rotation period is t_c, the forest is divided into $\frac{1}{t_c}$ areas, so that one area is available for harvest each year. To maximize

176 *A Brief Introduction to Traditional Forestry Economics*

the sustainable yield the rotation age t_c would still be chosen to maximize the mean annual increment.

A.5 Do Economies of Scale Require Large Tenures and Large Mills?

It is argued by some that the key to survival for the North American forestry industry is to exploit economies of scale. In Ontario, for example, both industry and the Ministry of Natural Resources have suggested that the most significant competition is coming from mills in areas where the plantation forests are said to be 50 times as productive as the boreal forest and the mills are many times larger. According to this technological scenario, small Ontario mills, for example, will have to close and timber will be diverted to supermills in the province that are more efficient.

The argument is not entirely convincing. Supplying larger mills requires much larger areas in Northern regions because trees grow more slowly. Larger areas result in much larger transportation costs than the plantation-based competitor mills.[6] Transportation costs increase with a multiple of the *square* of the distance, while the harvest only increases with a multiple of the distance. In effect, larger mills receive transportation subsidies because they use public highways more heavily. At the same time, supermills generally reduce employment per unit of wood processed.

More generally, it is unclear why sawmills must be very large when in many manufacturing industries, smaller scale, more flexible production systems are being developed. It is possible that the major economies of scale are not at the level of the mill's technology, but are largely a result of economies in management, political influence, financing and marketing. If larger companies have advantages because of information and social technologies, especially if those advantages arise from reduced transaction costs, most of the efficiencies might be achieved by networks of smaller producers with improved information technology and coordination. Information technology and coordination are rapidly getting cheaper.

A.6 Other Topics

Forestry economics is a mix of biology and management issues. It is not limited to the few core topics covered in this brief appendix. *The Journal of Forest Economics,* for example "publishes scientific papers in subject areas such as":

1. forest management problems: economics of silviculture, forest regulation and operational activities, managerial economics;
2. forest industry analysis: economics of processing, industrial organization problems, demand and supply analysis, technological change, international trade of forest products;
3. multiple use of forests: valuation of non-market priced goods and services, cost-benefit analysis of environment and timber production, external effects of forestry and forest industry;
4. forest policy analysis: market and intervention failures, regulation of forest management, ownership, taxation;
5. forestry and economic development: deforestation and land use problems, national resource accounting, contribution to national and regional income and employment.

In each of these areas there is a rich and important literature that deserves careful attention and will often illuminate issues in the economics of community forestry.

Notes

[1] "There is an optimal combination of stocking density and harvest age that will produce the highest value combination of volume and quality for each interaction of species and site. The specific prescription will depend on the desired end product." Jozsa and Middleton (1994)

[2] Figures very like Figure A.1 have been derived empirically for Scandinavian Boreal forests and for US temperate southern pine forest. The rotation period that yields MSY for the boreal forest MSY is 100 years, while for the temperate American forest it is about 30 years. Amacher, Ollikainen, and Koskela, 2009

[3] For an introduction on time discounting and present value calculations, see Appendix B.

[4] Tree size is the most important attribute affecting logging costs. Logging costs per unit of wood decrease significantly with increasing tree diameter and height. Holtzscher and Lanford, 1997

[5] Externalities were the subject of Chapter 7.

[6] It is easy to see how rapidly transportation costs increase using the formulae for the circumference of a circle. Increasing the radius of a circle by one unit increases the area by one times the circumference, or $2\pi r$. If a quantity of wood proportional to the area has to be transported to a mill at the centre of the circle, a distance r, total transportation costs increase in proportion to $r \times 2\pi r = 2\pi r^2$.

B
Time and Natural Resource Decisions

Optimal resource use is fundamentally about time. Resource problems typically involve inter-temporal choice: how best to allocate effort and resources across time. They can almost all be written in terms of maximizing the present value of the net benefits from owning a resource.

In almost every case, natural resource decisions today affect the amount of the resource available in the future. The special feature of a mine, for example, is that the amount of mineral wealth remaining at the end of each year is reduced by the amount harvested in that year. Biological stocks, often called renewable resources, are different. The stocks are reduced by harvesting, but they also increase naturally. The economics of renewable resources are particularly interesting because of the interaction between biology, economic process, and social/property relations.

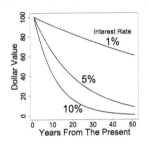

Figure B.1: Discounted value of $100

Maximizing the present value of an asset over time requires an understanding of the relationship between present and future values – which involves *discounting*.

180 *Time and Natural Resource Decisions*

B.1 Discounting

In general we **discount future benefits and costs**. Discounting is a complicated issue for many reasons. If you offer me one toffee today or two toffees in a year, I would take the toffee today even though waiting gives me a real rate of return of 100%. On the other hand, I am willing to accept a **nominal** rate of return of perhaps 2% on my retirement savings. This seems inconsistent, and it is, but in both cases I am discounting future benefits.

People do discount future benefits and costs, so we need a way to incorporate time and discounting into our analysis. We do it by using a trick, by restricting our framework to the case where our imaginary decision-makers are both rational and consistent and also have good capital markets.

A perfect capital market allows you to invest any sum and earn a known rate of return, say i % per year: the capital market will give you $(1 + i)$ dollars in a year for each dollar you put in today. What is happening here is that you are lending money to someone who wants it today and is promising to pay you for the use of your money. Obviously that someone expects to get at least $(1 + i)$ dollars in benefits or cash over the next year or she would not be willing to make that promise. The capital market is in effect moving money from people who think a dollar today is worth less than $(1 + i)$ tomorrow to people who think a dollar today is worth more than $(1 + i)$ tomorrow.

Capital markets are more complex of course – if you don't trust the borrower, or even if you just think the world might end – you would tend to ask for higher price. (The extra return you ask for in this case is called a **risk premium**.) It is also possible that prices will rise. When you get your $(1 + i)$ dollars in a year, prices might be $(1 + 2i)$ times the current level and you will actually be able to buy less with what you get. These are all complications worth thinking about, but it is a lot easier to understand the most basic principles of resource economics if we avoid dealing with inflation, uncertainty and imperfections in capital markets.

Discounting **181**

The assumption that we can lend or borrow at i % per year allows us to compute the values of revenue and costs at different times. We may want to know, for example, the **present value** of a dollar in two years. It will be discounted twice:

$$(dollar\ in\ two\ days) = \delta^2(dollar\ today)$$

If a dollar in 1 years= is only worth 0.9090909 dollars today, a dollar is two years is only worth 0.9090909 of a dollar in one year, or 0.8264463 of a dollar today.

The discount factor

If a dollar today buys you $(1 + i)$ dollars in a year, we can write

$$1(dollar\ today) = (1+i)(dollar\ tomorrow)$$
$$\frac{1}{1+i)}(dollar\ today) = (dollar\ tomorrow)$$

This says a dollar tomorrow is only worth $\frac{1}{1+i}$ dollars today.

The expression $\delta = \frac{1}{1+i}$ is the **discount factor**.

It is essentially the price today of money tomorrow.
For example if $i = 0.1$ is an interest rate of 10%, then $\delta = \frac{1}{1.1} = 0.9090909$. I say "Lend me a dollar – I'll have it back to you in a year." You say "Nope! A dollar in a year is only worth 91 cents to me at the current interest rate."

---

182 Time and Natural Resource Decisions

Going a step farther, The present values of a dollar in t years is

$$PV(dollar\ at\ time\ t) = \delta^t(dollar\ today)$$

where

$$\delta^t = \frac{1}{(1+i)^t} = 0.9090909^t$$

This gives us a price for any period, providing i is constant.

Do people really discount by simple compounding like this? Probably not reliably, but, if they don't, there are opportunities for arbitrage, and there are often sophisticated investors who do use the rule, and they will outperform those who don't.

It is a useful and almost ubiquitous formula. To see what it means in practical terms, think about what it tells you about taking care of grandchildren. Assume that we love our grandchildren as we love

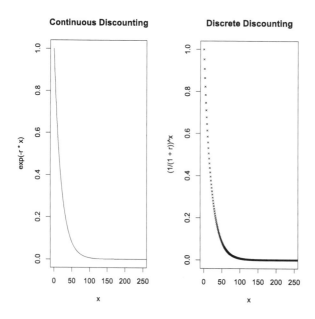

Figure B.2: Continuous and discrete discounting

ourselves. Then, as Richard B. Howarth (2003) points out, if we use a zero discount rate, we should be willing to pay up to $100 today to save $100 in cost for our grandchildren sixty years from now. If we use a discount rate of even 1 percent, the calculation indicates that we should not pay more than $55. Discounting at a 3 percent we shouldn't pay anything over $17. At a 5 percent rate the present value of $100 of pain for our grandchildren is only $5 to us.

B.2   Discrete and Continuous Discounting

The description above assumes that we want to treat time in segments of, for example, a year. We used a **discrete** discount factor,

$$\delta^t = \frac{1}{(1+i)^t}.$$

In this case t stands for the number of years and it has to be a whole number. Fractions are not allowed.

If we wanted to calculate the discount factor for transactions at arbitrary times, say 2.3765 years, we need a discount factor that is expressed in terms of the amount of time that has passed. We use a **continuous** discount factor,

$$\delta^t = e^{-rt}.$$

Figure B.2 shows that the two discount factors yield almost identical discount curves.

184 *Notes*

Notes

[1] "There is an optimal combination of stocking density and harvest age that will produce the highest value combination of volume and quality for each interaction of species and site. The specific prescription will depend on the desired end product." Jozsa and Middleton (1994)

[2] Figures very like Figure A.1 have been derived empirically for Scandinavian Boreal forests and for US temperate southern pine forest. The rotation period that yields MSY for the boreal forest MSY is 100 years, while for the temperate American forest it is about 30 years. Amacher, Ollikainen, and Koskela, 2009

[3] For an introduction on time discounting and present value calculations, see Appendix B.

[4] Tree size is the most important attribute affecting logging costs. Logging costs per unit of wood decrease significantly with increasing tree diameter and height. Holtzscher and Lanford, 1997

[5] Externalities were the subject of Chapter 7.

[6] It is easy to see how rapidly transportation costs increase using the formulae for the circumference of a circle. Increasing the radius of a circle by one unit increases the area by one times the circumference, or $2\pi r$. If a quantity of wood proportional to the area has to be transported to a mill at the centre of the circle, a distance r, total transportation costs increase in proportion to $r \times 2\pi r = 2\pi r^2$.

C
Definitions

Allowable Cut Effect (ACE) The increase in today's average annual allowable cut attributable to expected future increases in yields. Luckert and Haley (1995)

appurtenancy requirements The requirement that a forest licensee construct, modify or maintain a timber processing facility.

black liquor The waste product from the kraft process when digesting pulpwood into paper pulp, removing lignin, hemicelluloses and other substances from the wood to free the cellulose fibres. Now often used as a fuel. Valuable components may be recovered.

community A social group of any size whose members reside in a specific locality, share government, and often have a common cultural and historical heritage. From Anglo-Norman and Middle French communité, comunité, joint ownership (OED).

community forest A forest regarded as a resource for a local community (OED). For the purpose of this book, a decentralized and democratic form of public ownership of forests in which a resident community effectively owns the forest, depends on the forest for a significant fraction of its living, makes all the important decisions about forest resources, and captures all the benefits from forest use.

discount rate The rate at which future future benefits are discounted.

economies of scale Cost savings that arise when average costs can be reduced by increasing the *quantity* of output.

186 *Definitions*

economies of scope Cost savings that arise when average costs can be reduced by increasing the *variety* of outputs.

First Nation A term used in Canada for an aboriginal community, generally a tribe, usually on a treaty reserve.

indigenous communities Peoples and nations are those which, having a historical continuity with pre-invasion and pre-colonial societies that developed on their territories, consider themselves distinct from other sectors of the societies now prevailing on those territories, or parts of them. From the UN Study on the Problem of Discrimination against Indigenous Populations. Cobo (1982)

innovation network An innovation network is a group of agents (e.g., individuals, teams, organizations) that are connected via relationships that enable the exchange of information and/or other resources. Schilling (2014)

joint products Two or more outputs generated simultaneously, by a single manufacturing process using common inputs.

market failure any situation in which a perfectly free market fails to produce an efficient outcome.

Maximum Sustainably Yield (MSY) The largest harvest that can be extracted over an indefinite period. The maximum sustainable yield is usually higher than the optimum sustainable yield and maximum economic yield.

Mean Annual Increment (MAI) The average growth per year of a tree or stand of trees up to a specified age. Size divided by age.

merchantable timber Standing trees that have commercial value as millstock, a subset of the total timber stock.

Optimal Sustainable Yield (OSY) The level of harvest that maximizes the difference between total revenue and total cost. Compare to Maximum Sustainably Yield.

preference revelation problem The problem of ascertaining the public's demand for public goods if government planners do not have "full knowledge of individual preferences". It arises when individuals have an incentive to not reveal their true preferences.

regulatory capture A form of political corruption that occurs when a regulatory agency, created to act in the public interest, instead

Definitions **187**

advances the commercial or political concerns of special interest groups that dominate the industry or sector it is charged with regulating.

subsidiarity The principle that social problems should be dealt with at the most immediate (or local) level consistent with their solution.

tenure The conditions under which land or buildings are held or occupied. (OED)

time preference A preference for good things sooner rather than later. Sometimes a measure of the strength of that preference, i.e., to the rate of time preference. See *discount rate*.

transaction cost A cost incurred in making an economic exchange.

Bibliography

Adhikar, Bhim and Jon C. Lovett (2006). "Transaction costs and community-based natural resource management in Nepal". In: *Journal of Environmental Management* 78, pp. 5–15.

Agrawal, Arun and Jesse C. Ribot (1999). "Accountability in decentralization: A framework with South Asian and West African cases". In: *The Journal of Developing Areas*, pp. 473–502.

Ahuja, G. (2000). "Collaboration networks, structural holes, and innovation: A longitudinal study." In: *Administrative Science Quarterly* 45, pp. 425–455.

Allen, Douglas W. (2000). "Transaction Costs". In: *The Encyclopedia of Law and Economics*. Ed. by Boudewijn Bouckaert and Gerrit De Geest. Cheltenham: Edward Elgar, pp. 893–926.

Amacher, Gregory S., Markku Ollikainen, Erkki Koskela, et al. (2009). *Economics of Forest Resources*. Mit Press Cambridge.

Arnold, J. E. M. (2001). *Forests and People: 25 Years of Community Forestry*. Rome: FAO.

Arrow, Kenneth J. (1951). "An Extension of the Basic Theorems of Classical Welfare Economics". In: *Proceedings of the Second Berkeley Symposium on Mathematical Statistics and Probability*. Ed. by N. J. Neyman. Berkeley: University of California Press, pp. 507–532.

Arthur, Brian W. (2009). *The Nature of Technology: What it Is and How it Evolves*. Free Press, Simon & Schuster.

Auditor General, Ontario Office of the (2006). *Auditors Annual Report*.

Baker, Mark and Jonathan Kusel (2003). *Community Forestry in the United States: Learning from the past, crafting the future*. Island Press.

Barnett, A.H. and Bruce Yandle (2009). "The End of the Externality Revolution". In: *Social Philosophy and Policy* 26.2, pp. 130–150.

Baumgärtner, Stefan, Malte Faber, and Johannes Schiller (2006). *Joint Production and Responsibility in Ecological Economics: On the Foundations of Environmental Policy*. UK: Edward Elgar. Cheltenham.

Becker, Gary (1964). *Human Capital: A Theoretical and Empirical Analysis, with Special Reference to Education*. Chicago: University of Chicago Press.

Benner, Jordan, Ken Lertzman, and Evelyn W. Pinkerton (2014). "Social contracts and community forestry: How can we design forest policies and tenure arrangements to generate local benefits?" In: *Canadian Journal of Forest Research*. 44.8.

BLS (2015). *Occupational Outlook Handbook*. Tech. rep. Bureau of Labour Statistics, US Department of Labour.

Bourdieu, Pierre (1986). "The Forms of Capital". In: *Handbook of Theory and Research for the Sociology of Education*. Ed. by J Richardson. Greenwood, pp. 241–258.

Bowler, Diana E. et al. (2012). "Does community forest management provide global environmental benefits and improve local welfare?" In: *Frontiers in Ecology and the Environment* 10.1.

Bradshaw, Ben (2003). "Questioning the credibility and capacity of community-based resource management". In: *Canadian Geographer* 47.2, pp. 137–150.

Bray, David Barton et al. (2003). "Mexico's Community-Managed Forests as a Global Model for Sustainable Landscapes". In: *Conservation Biology* 17.3, pp. 672–677.

Brazee, R.J. and R. Mendelsohn (1988). "Timber Harvesting with Fluctuating Prices". In: *Forest Science* 34, pp. 359–372.

Brown, David S. and Wendy Hunter (2004). "Democracy and Human Capital Formation: Education Spending in Latin America, 1980 to 1997". In: *Comparative Political Studies* 37, pp. 842–864.

Buchy, Marlène and Digby Race (2001). "The Twists and Turns of Community Participation in Natural Resource Management in Australia: What is Missing?" In: *Journal of Environmental Planning and Management* 44.3, pp. 293–308.

Burdin, Gabriel (2014). "Are worker-managed firms more likely to fail than conventional enterprises?" In: *Evidence from Uruguay. Industrial & Labor Relations Review.* 67.1, pp. 202–238.

Burdin, Gabriel and Andrés Dean (2012). "Revisiting the objectives of worker-managed firms: An empirical assessment". In: *Economic Systems* 36.1, pp. 158–171.

Burt, R. S. (1992). *Structural Holes: The Social Structure of Competition.* Cambridge, MA: Harvard University Press.

– (1997). "The contingent value of social capital". In: *Administrative Science Quarterly* 42, pp. 339–365.

Castén, Tuukka (2005). "Ownership and Incentives in Joint Forest Management: A Survey". In: *Development Policy Review,* 23.1, pp. 87–104.

Charnley, Susan and Melissa R Poe (2007). "Community forestry in theory and practice: where are we now?" In: *Annual Review of Anthropology* 36.1, p. 301.

Cheung, Steven N. S (1969). *A Theory of Share Tenancy.* Chicago: University of Chicago Press.

Christopherson, Susan, Michael Kitson, and Jonathan Michie (2008). "Innovation, networks and knowledge exchange". In: *Cambridge Journal of Regions, Economy and Society* 1, pp. 165–173.

Clutter, Mike et al. (2005). *Strategic Factors Driving Timberland Ownership Changes in the US South.* USDA Forest Service, Southern Research Station, Research Triangle Park, NC.

Coase, Ronald H. (1937). "The nature of the firm". In: *Economica* 4, pp. 386–405.

– (1960). "The Institutional Structure of Production: Lecture to the memory of Alfred Nobel". In:

Cobo, Jose R. Martinez (1982). *Study on the Problem of Discrimination Against Indigenous Populations.* Final Report. United Nations Economic and Social Council Commission on Human Rights.

Coleman, J. (1990). *The Foundations of Social Theory.* Cambridge: Harvard University Press.

Commons, John R. (1931). "Institutional Economics". In: *American Economic Review* 21, pp. 648–657.

192 Bibliography

Cornejo, Carlos et al. "Opportunities and Challenges for Community forestry: Lessons from Tropical America". In: *Forests and Society: Responding to Global Driver of Change*. Ed. by Gerardo Mery et al. Vol. 25. IURFO.

Cote, S. and T. Healy (2001). *The Well-being of Nations. The Role of Human and Social Capital*. Tech. rep. Organisation for Economic Co-operation and Development, Paris.

Cox, M., G. Arnold, and S. V. Tomás (2010). "A review of design principles for community-based natural resource management". In: *Ecology and Society* 15.4 Art. 38.

Craig, Ben and John Pencavel (1993). "The objectives of worker cooperatives". In: *Journal of Comparative Economics* 17.2883, pp. 288–308.

Dahl, Henry G. (1957). *Worker-Owned Plywood Companies in the State of Washington*. Everett, Wash: Manuscript.

Dasgupta, Partha (2003). "Social Capital and Economic Performance: Analytics". In: *Foundations of Social Capital*. Ed. by Elizabeth Ostrom and T. Ahn. mimeo, Faculty of Economics, University of Cambridge. Cheltenham: Edward Elgar, pp. 309–339.

Deacon, Robert T (1999). "Deforestation and ownership: evidence from historical accounts and contemporary data". In: *Land Economics*, pp. 341–359.

Dodd, Peter Sheridan, Roby Muhamad, and Duncan J. Watts (2003). "An Experimental Study of Search in Global Social Networks". In: *Science* 301.5634, p. 827.

Dombeck, M. and A. Moad (2001). "Forests and the future: regional perspectives – North America." In: *Unasylva* 204, pp. 49–51.

Doucouliagos, Chris (1995). "Worker Participation and Productivity in Labor-Managed and Participatory Capitalist Firms: A Meta-Analysis". In: *Industrial and Labor Relations Review*. 1, pp. 58–77.

Dow, Gregory K. and Louis Putterman (2000). "Why capital suppliers (usually) hire workers: what we know and what we need to know". In: *Journal of Economic Behavior & Organization* 43, pp. 319–336.

Dressler, Wolfram H., Melanie H. McDermott, and Carsten Schusser. "The politics of community forestry in a Global Age – A critical analysis". In: *Forest Policy and Economics: Special Issue on Community Forestry* 58.2015, pp. 1–4.

Duane, T. P. (1977). "Community participation in ecosystems management". In: *Ecology Law Quarterly* 24, pp. 771–797.

Dudwick, Nora et al. (2006). *Analyzing Social Capital in Context: A Guide to Using Qualitative Methods and Data*. Tech. rep. Washington D.C.: World Bank Institute.

Duinker, Peter N. et al. (1994). "Community Forests in Canada: An Overview". In: *Forestry Chronicle*. 70.6, pp. 131–135.

Durlauf, Steven N. and Marcel Fafchamps (2004). *Social Capital*. Tech. rep. National Bureau of Economic Research.

Fakhfakh, Fathi, Virginie Perotin, and Monica Gago (2012). "Productivity, capital and labour in labour-managed and conventional firms: an investigation on French data". In: *Industrial & Labor Relations Review*. 65.4, pp. 847–879.

Fleming, L., C. King, and A. Juda (2007). "Small worlds and regional innovation". In: *Organization Science* 18, pp. 938–954.

Flint, Courtney G., A. E. Luloff, and James C. Finley (2008). "Where Is "Community" in Community-Based Forestry?" In: *Society & Natural Resources* 21.6, pp. 526–537.

Gamble, Alfred (forthcoming). "The Junior Forest Rangers Program in Northern Saskatchewan". In: *Bridging Practice, Research and Advocacy for Community Forests in Canada*. Ed. by Ryan Bullock et al. University of Manitoba Press.

Gilpin, A. (2000). *Environmental Economics: A Critical Overview*. Chichester, UK (cit in Kumar, Kumar 2008): Wiley.

Glasmeier, Amy K. and Tracey Farrigan (2005). "Understanding community forestry: a qualitative meta-study of the concept, the process, and its potential for poverty alleviation in the United States case". In: *Geographical Journal* 171.1, pp. 56–69.

Gordon, H. Scott (1954). "The Economic Theory of a Common-Property Resource: The Fishery". In: *Journal of Political Economy* 62.2, pp. 124–142.

194 *Bibliography*

Guiang, E. S., S. B. Borlagdan, and J. M. Pulhin (2001). *Community-based Forest Management in the Philippines: a preliminary assessment*. Project Report. Quezon City, Institute of Philippine Culture, Ateneo de Manila University.

Gunter, Jennifer and Lisa Ambus (2004). "Welcome to the Community Forestry Guidebook". In: *The Community Forestry Guidebook: Tools and Techniques for Communities in British Columbia*. Ed. by Jennifer Gunter. 15. FOREX.

Hamid, O. (2004). "Curriculum revision for sustainable forest resource management in southern Africa". In: *unsylva* 55.1, pp. 24–25.

Hanifan, L. J. (1916). "The rural school community center". In: *Annals of the American Academy of Political and Social Science*.

Hansmann, H. (1988). "Ownership of the firm". In: *Journal of Law, Economics, and Organization* 4.2, pp. 267–305.

Harrington, Chris, Allan Curtis, and Rosemary Black (2008). "Locating Communities in Natural Resource Management". In: *Journal of Environmental Policy & Planning* 10.2, pp. 199–215.

Harshaw, H. W. (2000). "Development of the Community Forest Tenure in British Columbia: An Examination of the BCMoF Community Forestry Initiative". PhD thesis. University of British Columbia.

Hartman, Richard (1976). "The harvesting decison when a standing forest has value". In: *Economic Inquiry* 14.1, pp. 52–58.

Harvey, D. (1996). *Justice, Nature and the Geography of Difference*. Cambridge, UK: Blackwell.

Hirsch, F., A. Korotkov, and M. Wilnhammer (2007). "Private forest ownership in Europe". In: *Unasylva* 228.

Holling, C.S. (1973). "Resilience and stability of ecological systems". In: *Annual review of ecology and systematics*, pp. 1–23.

– (1986). "The resilience of terrestrial ecosystems; local surprise and global change". In: *Sustainable development of the biosphere*. Ed. by W.C. Clark and R.E. Munn. Cambridge, UK: Cambridge University Press.

Holtzscher, Matthew A. and Bobby L. Lanford (1997). "Tree Diameter Effects on Cost and Productivity of Cut-to-Length Systems". In: *Forest Products Journal* 47.3.

Howarth, Richard B. (2003). "Discounting and Uncertainty in Climate Change Policy Analysis". In: *Land Economics* 79.3, pp. 369–381.

Inkpen, Andrew C. and Eric W. K. Tsang (2005). "Social Capital, Networks, and Knowledge Transfer". In: *The Academy of Management Review* 1, pp. 146–165.

Insight, LMI and R.A. Matatest & Associates (2013). *British Columbia Forest Sector Labour Market & Training Needs Analysis: Final Report*. Tech. rep. BC Coastal Forest Industry Labour Market Information Working Group.

Jacobs, Jane (1961). *The Death and Life of Great American Cities*. Random House.

Jensen, Michael C. and William H. Meckling (1976). "Theory of the Firm: Managerial Behavior, Agency Costs and Ownership Structure". In: *Journal of Financial Economics* 3.4, pp. 305–360.

Jong, Wil de et al. (2010). "Opportunities and Challenges for Community forestry: Lessons from Tropical America". In: *Forests and Society: Responding to Global Driver of Change*. Ed. by Gerardo Mery et al. Vol. 25. IURFO World Series no. 25. IURFO.

Jozsa, L.A. and G.R. Middleton (1994). *A Discussion of Wood Quality Attributes and Their Practical Implications*. Special Publication SP-34. Forintek.

Kant, Shashi (2009). "Global Trends in Ownership and Tenure of Forest Resources and Timber Pricing". Prepared for the Ontario Professional Foresters Association.

Kim, Seong-il (2014). "Experience of ASEAN and ROK Cooperation on Forest Education and Some Thoughts for Future". In: vol. Forestry Education and Research in Asia: Reality, Challeneges, and Way forward. Forest Asia. CIFOR.

Krutilla, John V. (1967). "Conservation Reconsidered". In: *American Economic Review*, 57.4, pp. 777–786.

Kumar, M. and P. Kumar (2008). "Valuation of ecosystem services: a psycho-cultural perspective". In: *Ecological Economics* 64, pp. 808–819.

Laffont, Jean-Jacques and Jean Tirole (1991). "The politics of government decision-making: A theory of regulatory capture". In: *The Quarterly Journal of Economics*, pp. 1089–1127.

Lakany, Hosny El (2014). "Needed: a new forestry graduate". In: *Forestry Education and Research in Asia: Reality, Challenges, and Way forward*. ASEAN-ROK Forest Cooperation Secretariat. CIFOR.

Larson, Anne M. et al. (2008). *Tenure Rights and Beyond: Community Access to Forest Resources in Latin America*. ocassional paper 50. Bogor Barat, Indonesia: Center for International Forestry Research (CIFOR).

Lawson, Jamie, Marcelo Levy, and L. Anders Sandberg (2001). "Change, Continuity and Forest Policy Regimes in Ontario". In: *Canadian Forest Policy: Adapting to Change*. Ed. by Michael Howlett. Toronto: University of Toronto press.

Luckert, Martin K. (1999). "Are Community forests the key to sustainable forest management? Some economic considerations". In: *Forestry Chronicle* 75.5.

– (2009). *Considering Privatization in Canada's Forest Tenures*. Tech. rep. Presented to the Ontario Professional Foresters Association April 23, 2009, Sudbury, Ontario.

Luckert, Martin K. and D. Haley (1995). "The allowable cut effect as a policy instrument in Canadian forestry". In: *Canadian Journal of Forest Resources* 25, pp. 1821–1829.

Mallik, Azim U. and Hafizur Rahman (1994). "Community forestry in developed and developing countries: A comparative study". In: *The Forestry Chronicle* 70.6, pp. 731–735.

McDermott, M. H. and Kate Schreckenberg (2009). "Equity in community forestry: insights from North and South". In: *International Forestry Review* 11.2, pp. 157–170.

Meshack, Charles K. et al. (2006). "Transaction costs of community-based forest management: empirical evidence from Tanzania". In: *African Journal of Ecology* 44, pp. 468–477.

Miller, H. (2004). "Trends in forestry education in Great Britain and Germany, 1992 to 2001". In: *Unasylva* 55.216, pp. 29–32.

Mincer, Jacob (1958). "Investment in human capital and personal income distribution". In: *Journal of Political Economy* 66, pp. 281–302.

Miyazaki, Hajime and Hugh M. Neary (1983). "The Illyrian Firm Revisited". In: *The Bell Journal of Economics*. 14.1, pp. 259–270.

Moazzami, B. (2006). *An Economic Impact Analysis of the Northwestern Ontario Forest Sector*. Tech. rep. Northwestern Ontario Forest Council.

Moote, Margaret A. and Dennis R. Becker (2004). "Community Forestry in the United States: Learning from the Past, Crafting the Future, by Mark Baker and Jonathan Kusel". In: *Rural Sociology* 69.1, pp. 161–164.

Nair, C.T.S (2004). "What does the future hold for forestry education?" In: *Unasylva* 55.216, pp. 3–9.

Nelson, Harry (2008). *Alternative Tenure Approaches to Achieve Sustainable Forest Management: Lessons for Canada*. Tech. rep. Knowledge Exchange and Technology Extension Program (KETE) Sustainable Forest Management Network.

North, Douglas C. and R.P. Thomas (1973). *The Rise of the Western World: A New Economic History*. Cambridge, UK.: Cambridge University Press.

Ohlin, Bertil (1995). "Concerning the Question of the Rotation Period in Forestry". In: *Journal of Forest Economics* 1, pp. 89–114.

OMNR (2009). *Annual Report on Forest Management 2009/10*. Tech. rep. Ontario Ministry of Natural Resources.

Ostrom, Elinor (1990). *Governing the Commons*. Cambridge, UK: Cambridge University Press.

– (1995). "Designing Complexity to Govern Complexity and the Environment". In: *Property Rights and the Environment: Social and Ecological Issues, Volume 94*. Ed. by Susan Hanna and Mohan Munasinghe. Washington D.C.: Beijer International Institute of Ecological Economics and World Bank.

Ostrom, Elinor (2000). "Social Capital: a fad or a fundamental concept?" In: *Social Capital: A Multifaceted Perspective*. Ed. by Partha Dasgupta and I. Seragilden. World Bank, pp. 172–214.

– (2005). *Understanding Institutional Diversity*. Princeton, NJ: Princeton University Press.

Ostrom, Elinor et al. (1999). "Revisiting the Commons: Local Lessons, Global Challenges". In: *Science* 284.5412, pp. 278–28.

Owen-Smith, J. and W. W. Powell (2004). "Knowledge networks in the Boston biotechnology community , 15: 5–21". In: *Organization Science* 15, pp. 5–21.

Owen-Smith, J., M. Riccaboni, et al. (2002). "A comparison of U.S. and European university-industry relations in the life sciences." In: *Management Science* 48, pp. 24–43.

Pagdee, Adcharaporn, Yeon-su Kim, and P. J. Daugherty (2006). "What makes community forest management successful: a meta-study from community forests throughout the world". In: *Society and Natural Resources* 19.1, pp. 33–52.

Palmer, Lynn and Peggy Smith (forthcoming). "Transformative Community Organizing for Community forests in Northern Ontario: The Northern Ontario Sustainable Communities Partnership". In: *Bridging Practice, Research and Advocacy for Communities and their Forests in Canada*. Ed. by Ryan Bullock et al. University of Manitoba Press.

Pearse, Peter H. (1990). *Introduction to forestry economics*. UBC Press.

Pigou, Arthur Cecil (1928). *A Study in Public Finance*. Macmillan.

Pimentel, David et al. (1997). "The value of forests to world food security". In: *Human Ecology* 25.1, pp. 91–120.

Piore, Michael J. and Charles F. Sabel (1984). *The Second Industrial Divide*. New York: Basic Books.

Portes, Alejandro and Julia Sensenbrenner (1993). "Embeddedness and immigration: Notes on the social determinants of economic action". In: *American journal of sociology*, pp. 1320–1350.

Poteete, Amy R. and Jesse C. Ribot (2010). "Repertoires of Domination in Decentralization: Cases from Botswana and Senegal". In: *World Development* 39.3, pp. 439–449.

Powell, W. W. (1990). "Neither market nor hierarchy: Network forms of organization". In: *Research in Organizational Behavior 12*. Ed. by B. M. Staw and L. L. Cummings. Greenwich, CT: JAI Press., pp. 295–336.

Powell, Walter W., Kenneth W. Koput, and Laurel Smith-Doerr (1996). "Interorganizational Collaboration and the Locus of Innovation: Networks of Learning in Biotechnology". In: *Administrative Science Quarterly 41*, pp. 116–145.

Price, Colin (2011). "Optimal rotation with declining discount rate". In: *Journal of Forest Economics 17*, pp. 307–318.

Putnam, Robert D. (2000). *Bowling Alone: The Collapse and Revival of American Community*. Simon and Schuste.

Putnam, Robert D., R. Leonardi, and R. Nanetti (1993). *Making Democracy Work: Civic Traditions in Modern Italy*. Princeton, N.J.: Princeton University Press.

Rath, Bikash (2010). *Redefining Community Forestry for a Better Approach and a Better World*. Tech. rep. International Unionof Forest Research Organizations, Working Party on Community Forestry.

Ratnasingam, Jegatheswaran et al. (2013). "The Future of Professional Forestry Education: Trends and Challenges from the Malaysian Perspective". In: *Notulae Botanicae Horti Agrobotanici Cluj-Napoca* 41.1, pp. 12–20.

Reed, William J. (1985). "Optimal harvesting Models in Forest Management –A Survey".

Reed, William J. and D. Errico (1986). "Optimal harvest scheduling at the forest level in the presence of the risk of fire". In: *Canadian Journal of Forest Research* 16.2, pp. 266–278.

Richards, R. D. (1926). "The Early History of the Term Capital". In: *Quarterly Journal of Economics* 40.2.

Ritala, Paavo, Devi R Gnyawali, and Kati Helena Järvi (2014). "Configuration of Innovation Networks: A Conceptual Framework". In: *Academy of Management Proceedings*. Vol. 2014. 1. Academy of Management, p. 15063.

Roberts, Eryl H. and Madan K. Gautam (2003). *Community forestry lessons for Australia: a review of international case studies*. Research report. Canberra: School of Reosurces, Environment and Society, Australian National University.

Robinson, David and Kirsten Wright (2015). "A network approach to the innovation potential of community forestry". Prepared for the Annual conference of the Atlantic Canada Economics Association October 23-25th, 2015 at Wolfville, NS.

Rodríguez, R. Rojas (2004). "Professional forestry education and forestry development in Central America". In: *Unasylva* 55.216, pp. 33–37.

Rudebjer, P. G. and I. Siregar (2004). "Trends in forestry education in Southeast Asia and Africa, 1993 to 2002: preliminary results of two surveys". In: *Unasylva* 55.216.

Salisbury, Robert H. (1969). "An Exchange Theory of Interest Groups". In: *Midwest Journal of Political Science* 13.1, pp. 1–32.

Samuelson, Paul A. (1954). "The Pure Theory of Public Expenditure". In: *Review of Economics and Statistics* 36.4, pp. 387–389.

– (1976). "Economics of forestry in an evolving society". In: *Economic Inquiry* 14, pp. 466–492.

Saxenian, A. (1994). *Regional Advantage: Culture and Competition in Silicon Valley and Route 128*. Cambridge, MA: Harvard University Press.

Scherr, S., A. White, and D. Kaimowitz. (2004). *A new agenda for forest conservation and poverty reduction. Making markets work for forest communities*. Tech. rep.

Schilling, Melissa (2014). "innovation networks". In: *Palgrave Encyclopedia of Strategic Management*. Ed. by Mie Augier and David J. Teece. Palgrave.

Schusser, Carsten (2012). "Community Forestry: a Namibian Case Study". In: *Moving Forward With Forest Governance*. Ed. by G. Broekhoven, H. Svanije, and S. von Scheliha. Wageningen: Trobenbos International, pp. 213–221.

Sills, Erin O. and Karen Lee Abt (2003). "Introduction to *Forests in a Market Economy*". In: *Springer-Science+Business Media* Forestry Sciences Series.

Singh, Vijai Shanker, Deep Narayan Pandey, and Neha Pandey Prakash (2011). "What determines the success of joint forest management? Science-based lessons on sustainable governance of forests in India". In: *Resources, Conservation and Recycling* 56.1, pp. 126–133.

Skutsch, Margaret M. (2004). *Reducing carbon transaction costs in community based forest management*. Tech. rep. University of Twente: Technology and Sustainable Development Section.

Solo, Robert M. (2000). "Notes on Social Capital and Economic Performance". In: *Social Capital: A Multifaceted Perspective*. Ed. by Partha Dasgupta and I. Seragilden. World Bank, pp. 6–12.

Song, Shuang, Xiangdong Chen, and Gupeng Zhang (2014). "Structure of Small World Innovation Network and Learning Performance". In: *Mathematical Problems in Engineering* 2014.

Spangenberg, Joachim H. and Josef Settele (2010). "Precisely incorrect? Monetising the value of ecosystem services". In: *Ecological Complexity* 7, pp. 327–337.

Stasavage, David (2005). "Democracy and Education Spending in Africa". In: *American Journal of Political Science* 49.2, pp. 343–358.

Stigler, George (1971). "The theory of economic regulation". In: *Bell Journal of Economics and Management Science* 2.1, pp. 3–21.

Stuart, T. E., H. Hoang, and R. Hybels (1999). "Interorganizational endorsements and the performance of entrepreneurial ventures." In: *Administrative Science Quarterly* 44, pp. 315–349.

Suharti, Sri (2001). "Increased community participation in forest management through the development of social forestry programmes in Indonesia". In: *The Balance between Biodiversity Conservation and Sustainable Use of Tropical Rain Forests*. The Tropenbos Foundation, Wageningen, the Netherlands.

Sunderlin, W., J. Hatcher, and M. Liddle (2008). *From exclusion to ownership? Challenges and opportunities in advancing forest tenure reform*. Tech. rep. Washington DC: Rights and Resources Initiative.

Taylor, Curtis R. (2000). "The Old-Boy Network and the Young-Gun Effect". In: *International Economic Review* 41.4, pp. 871–891.

Temperate Forest Foundation (2006). "Forests as Financial Assets". In: *Ecolink* 15:1, p. 8.

Uzzi, B. (1997). "Social structure and competition in interfirm networks: The paradox of embedd". In: *Administrative Science Quarterly* 42, pp. 35–67.

Vega, Dora Carias and Rodney J. Keenan (2014). "Transaction cost theory of the firm and community forestry enterprises". In: *Forest Policy and Economics* 42, pp. 1–7.

Vertinsky, Ilan and Marty Luckert (2010). *Design of Forest Tenure Institutions: The Challenges of Governing Forests*. Tech. rep. Edmonton: Sustainable Forest Management Network.

Ward, Benjamin (1958). "The Firm in Illyria: Market Syndicalism". In: *The American Economic Review* 48.4, pp. 566–589. ISSN: 00028282.

Wasswa-Matovu, Joseph (2010). *The Effects of Transaction Costs on Community Forestry Management in Uganda*. Ethiopia: OSSREA.

Watts, Duncan J. and S. H. Strogatz (1998). "Collective dynamics of 'small-world' networks". In: *Nature* 393, pp. 440–442.

Whiteman, Adrian (2003). "Money doesn't grow on trees: a perspective on prospects for making forestry pay". In: *Unasylva* 54.212.

Whiteman, Adrian, Anoja Wickramasinghe, and Leticia Piña (2015). "Global trends in forest ownership, public income and expenditure on forestry and forestry employment". In: *Forest Ecology and Management* 352. Changes in Global Forest Resources from 1990 to 2015, pp. 99–108.

Williamson, Oliver E. (2010). "Transaction Cost Economics: The Natural Progression". In: *Journal of Retailing* 86.3, pp. 215–226.

World Resources Institute (2005). *Millennium Ecosystem Assessment*. Tech. rep. World Resources Institute.

Zhang, Daowei and Peter H. Pearse (1997). "The influence of form of the tenure on reforestation in British Columbia". In: *Forest Ecology and Management*. 98, pp. 239–250.

Zhang, S. Y. (2003). *Wood Quality Attributes and their Impact on Wood Utilization*. Tech. rep. XII World Forestry Congress.

Zhang, Y. (2001). "Economics of transaction costs saving forestry". In: *Ecological Economics* 36, pp. 197–204.

Index

AI, 164
Allowable Cut Effect
  definition, 185
argmax, 76
Arrow, Kenneth, 69

balanced tree, 121
bankruptcy, 137
bargaining, 112
bioeconomics, 161
boundaries, 6
Bourdieu, 63, 66

CAI, 164
canoe, 42
capacity building,
  114
capital, xxii, 66
  extensions of, 56
  features, 56
  financial, 59
  historic sense, 55
  human, 31, 34,
    60–62, 74, 114,
    137, 138
  natural, 60
  produced, 56
  real, 56
  social, 31, 34, 74

types of, 58
capitalism, 55, 60
carbon sequestration,
  42, 65, 83
carbon tax, 84
CBFM, *see*
  community-
  based forest
  management
choice modelling, 51
Clean Development
  Mechanism, 86
climate change, 65
community capacity,
  31
community forest
  decentralization, 5
  democracy, 5
  devolution, 7
  pure model, 3
community forestry
  definition, 3
  efficiency of, 67
  Fundamental
    Theorems, 68
community-based
  forest manage-
  ment, 105
comparative statics,

143
compliance, 113
compliance costs, 27
conjoint analysis, 51
constraint, 72
constraint, feasible,
  71
contingent valuation,
  51
contracting, 112
culmination age, 167

Debreu, Gerrard, 69
decentralization, 5
democracy, 5
derived demand (for
  foresters), 142
development, 29, 31,
  34, 70
discounting, 29, 30,
  179
  variable rate, 30
district heating, 119
diversification, 136

economies
  of scale, 107, 176
  of scope, 77, 111
ecosystem services,

42, 47–49, 83
efficiency
marginal con-
dition for,
85
employment, 134,
135
enforcement, 113
environmental
services, 43
excludability, 93
exogenous shock,
143
external benefits, 81
external costs, 81
externality, 50, 74, 81,
81–88, 98, 175
global warming,
82
inter-community,
86
internalizing, 82
intra-community,
87
negative, 81
NGOs, 87
positive, 83
property rights, 84
water quality, 83

fairness, 70
Faustmann, 170
Faustmann equation,
171
Faustmann model,
170–175
changing prices,
174
harvest costs, 174
feasible set, 25
financial maturity,

171
fire, 170
First Fundamental
Theorem of Wel-
fare Economics,
69
assumptions, 69
First Nations, 108
forest management
plan
economy of scale,
109
transaction cost,
109
forest-level manage-
ment, 175
forestry economics,
xvii
free-rider, 97
free-rider problem,
98
Fundamental Prop-
erty
first, 73
second, 73, 77
third, 77

global warming, 84
Gordon, Scott, 84
graph, 122

habitat, 42
Hartman model, 175
hedonic price, 51
human capital, 5, 44,
63
seecapital, human,
23

incentives, xxi
indigenous commu-

nities
UN definition, 22
indigenous peoples,
3, 17
industrial forestry
decreasing popula-
tion, 45
inflation, 31, 180
innovation, xxiii, 117
as treasure hunt,
123
labour replacing,
119
institutional eco-
nomics, 104
instrument-making,
120

job creation, 74
joint product, 42, 44,
47
and externalities,
41
and publicness, 41
as cause of envi-
ronmental
problems, 42
unpriced, 42
joint production, 29,
32, 41, 50

labour-replacing
technological
change, 45
liability, 100
local knowledge, 124
local public good
congestible, 94

MAI, *see* Maximum
Annual Incre-

Index 205

ment
marginal, **86**
  benefit, 85
  cost, 85, 86
  effects, 86
marginal benefit, 95, 96
marginal conditions, 71
marginal cost, 95
market distortion, 109, 110
market failure, 81, 83, 99
  beneficiary pays, 83
  polluter pays, 83
Marx, 44
Maximum Annual Increment, 166, 167, 169
Maximum Sustainable Yield, 166
mean annual increment, 164
membership, 6
mergers, 107
monitoring, 113
MSY, 166, 172
mushrooms, 42
Mystic Management, 108

natural resource management
  interest-based, 5
  place-based, 5
neoliberalism, 44
network, xxiii
NGO, *see* non-governmental

organizations
non-governmental organizations, 87
non-market transactions, 113
non-marketed goods, 49
non-monetary
  benefits, 86
  costs, 86
non-timber forest products, 111
normal forest, 176
norms, 58, 114

objective function, 71, 72
open-access fishery, 84
option value, 50, 100

Pareto efficiency, 68, 70, 106
Pareto improvement, 69
Philippines, 17, 22
Pigou, A.C, 84
Pigouvian tax, 84, 87
PPF, 26
preference revelation problem, 96, 97
present value
  calculation of, 181
process innovation, 118
productivity, 138
proportional annual increment, 164
public good, 41
  broadcaster, 93

chapter, 91
congestion, 94
definition, 91
local, 98–100
nonexcludability, 92
nonrivarousness, 92
roads, 94

rate of growth, 165
recreation, 111
REDD, 83, 86
regeneration, 44
regulatory capture, 27
revealed preference, 51
revenue growth, 165
risk, 136
risk premium, 180

Samuelson, 95, 96
self-employment, 120
sequestration, 111
small world, xxiii, 117
  characteristics, 122
small world network, 122
Smith, Adam, 67
social capital, 62, 63
  and community Forestry, 64
  and OECD, 63
  and World Bank, 64
  seecapital, social, 23
social reproduction,

44
social welfare, 71
stated preference,
     see contingent
     valuation
supermills, 176
sustainable forestry,
     44

TCT, *see* transaction
     cost theory
tenure, 23–42
  conventional, 44
tenure), 37
Thailand, 22
threat point, 113
time, 179
time preference, 170
tourism, 111
transaction
  cost, 109
transaction cost, 110

bargaining, 111
chapter on, 103
external, 111
search, 111
theory, 103
transaction cost
     theory, 106
transaction costs
  enforcement, 112
  forest manage-
     ment plan,
     109
  internal, 111
transportation costs,
     176
travel cost method,
     51
trust, 113, 114

value
  intrinsic, 52
  market, 52

non-use value, 52
option, 52
present value, 52
quasi-option, 52
use value, 52
vicarious, 52
value-added, 45, 132
  definition, 45
vertical integration,
     107

welfare economics
Fundamental
     Theorem, 67
welfare maximiza-
     tion, 71
welfarism, 70
WMF, *see* worker-
     managed firm
worker-managed
     firm, 133–139
WRI, 22